ADGE

KING OF THE WURZELS

John Hudson

BRISTOL BOOKS

BRISTOL BOOKS CIC

Unit 5.16 Paintworks, Bath Road, Bristol BS4 3EH

Bristol Books CIC was formed in 2012 by author and broadcaster
Clive Burlton, designer Joe Burt, Richard Jones of Tangent Books
and Martin Powell of Empica PR

ISBN 978-1-909446-01-4

Copyright: John Hudson/Bristol Books

John Hudson has asserted his right under the Copyright, Designs
and Patents Act of 1988 to be identified as the author of this work.

First Edition printed by Short Run Press, Exeter, November 2012,
reprinted January 2013

A CIP record for this book is available from the British Library

 **BRISTOL BOOKS**

Bristol Books CIC is a not-for-profit Community Interest Company that publishes important and untold stories about lives, communities, places and events that have significance and interest in Bristol and the surrounding area

ABOUT THE AUTHOR

John Hudson is the author, compiler or editor of more than thirty books of social history, regional interest and biography.

Dedication

This book is dedicated to two men too young to have seen Adge Cutler live, but whose commitment to and love of his work will help keep his legacy alive for many years to come. Raise your jars and Drink Up Thy Zider to Jonathan Conibere and Luke Hebden

Contents

Saturday May 4, 1974

Live every day as if it were your last, they say, and if he had known then what we know now, Adge Cutler would have spent his last twenty-four hours on earth in a different way. A sell-out concert at the Royal Albert Hall, perhaps, or up on stage at some sunny early summer festival, beating time with his Wurzel stick and leading a hundred thousand happy faces in a raucous *Drink Up Thy Zider*. Maybe, but almost certainly it would have been neither of these, and the day would have been spent on the Atlantic coast of Basque Spain, sharing red wine and tapas with loved ones and friends as the sun sank into the ocean and the fireflies danced around.

None of that was to be, but if he had looked back at the end of his show at twelve o'clock that Saturday night, oblivious to what was to come before dawn, he would surely have thought yes, that was a good day, that was all right. It is as much as any of us can hope for.

It was a decent morning to be out in the garden, and he welcomed that, because he loved it and had great plans for it. He had bought Craigie Knoll on Tickenham Hill as a bit of a snip at £10,000 a couple of years earlier, and Adge always liked a bit of a snip. His brother Roy was doing some house clearance work at the time, and an estate agent had tipped him off that this one was coming on the market. Now Adge wanted to create the kind of setting he believed the house deserved. Its arches, pantiles and balcony would not have looked out of place on the Spanish coast; in truth, they would have looked more in place there than they did in rural North Somerset, or Woodspring, in Avon, as he had refused to call it since April 1. As for its location, it was all Adge had ever aspired to. 'See those houses up there on the hill,' he once told his little brother Dave. 'That's where I'm going to live one day.'

'It was one of his dreams, and it was one that came true,' Dave Cutler says today, and once Adge landed his house on the hill he shared his satisfaction at fulfilling his fantasy to live up there with several other people, including his band mate Tommy Banner. Roy Cutler, on the other hand, had never heard the story. 'As far as I was concerned, it was a house that had become available, and it was the luck of the draw that he got it,' he says. Bearing in mind its location, 'serendipity' might be a better word.

With him in the garden that morning was John Tucker, building ornamental stone walls. He was an old Nailsea pal, half a dozen years younger than Adge, and Craigie Knoll was proving quite a good little project for him. He had already put up the tall gateposts at the bottom of the drive, and there was talk of other work in the offing.

'It was when Coate's were closing in Nailsea, and Adge was interested in the cider vat named after him to commemorate the time he worked there,' says John. Now it would not be needed any more, he hoped to get hold of it and put it up towards his woodlands at the back of the garden, turned upside-down and converted into a summer house. This, of course, would have displayed the bold white legend 'Adge Cutler And The Wurzels' the wrong way up, but this was of no immediate concern to the two men as they walked up to the proposed site. Adge's wife of two years, Yvonne, was expecting friends to visit and was back at the house.

'Later in the morning we went in his van to the Holms sand and gravel company in Hotwells to find a suitable surfacing for his drive,' John recalls. 'Its wharf was the base for sand dredgers operating out of Bristol City Docks in the Severn Estuary – around Flat Holm and Steep Holm, in fact – before they relocated to Avonmouth. As we were ordering what Adge wanted, the chap behind the counter kept looking at him in an odd kind of way. In the end he said "You're that one who's been on the telly with the funny hat, ain't you?"'

After this cheering encounter – Adge liked to be recognised, if only for his funny hat – he decided he wanted to go for some chitterling, those delectable pigs' intestines celebrated in more than one of his songs. 'He really did like it as much as he reckoned,' says John. 'He took us to a little old shop in Bedminster and came out with a pound of it and a Bath chap. He said he was saving that for Sunday, but we sat in the van eating the chitterling out of the paper.' Going back via the King's Head in Pill, the riverside community Adge saw as his second home, the two men enjoyed a leisurely pint over half an hour before going their separate ways. For Adge it was home to watch the Liverpool-Newcastle Cup Final on TV, and nobody expected anything other than a routine win for the Reds. So it proved, and a quiet, non-stressful afternoon in front of the telly suited Adge well enough. In an hour or so, for the sixth and last time in the week, he would be heading over the Severn Bridge and up through the Wye Valley to Hereford, where the Wurzels' cabaret stint at the Crystal Room had been going down a storm.

He liked Hereford, cider country to rival Somerset. All week long there had been Bulmers people in the audience, and they had welcomed him as one of their own – his kind of folk, in contrast to the crowds in the big cities in the North and Midlands, where he was never at his ease. The journey would be a bit of a pain, not to mention yet another 12.5p toll – fifteen bob a week, just to go over a bridge! But he knew that once he was up there all would be well, and apart from the buzz and good humour of the club, before his work began he looked forward to dropping in on his favourite town centre pub, the Orange Tree. Its Football League ref landlord Jacko Williams would doubtless be fulminating over the Liverpool full-back Lindsay's wrongly disallowed net-buster – one of Wembley's 'greatest goals that never were' – and there would be some good banter there.

Before Adge left, John Tucker phoned to tell him he had arranged for a man to come round the following day to measure up for some wrought-iron window box frames. He laughed with that odd, wheezy, gravelly chuckle of his, and said John had caught him tucking into the Bath chap that was supposed to last him until Sunday. Another call was to his manager, John Miles: 'Adge rang me every single day: "Johnner, just checking in." He called at 5.30 that night, after the Cup Final, and said "I'm driving up there tonight, I'm not going with the bandwagon." And that's what he did.'

After checking in at the Crystal Room – that 'Room' had become 'Rooms' by the time the club closed in 2003 – Adge and the band made their way the couple of hundred yards up the road to the pub, where Jacko's welcoming crowd usually included his wife, daughters Anne and Jackie and Philip Morris, a young man they had taken in almost as part of the family after his mother had died one Christmas Eve. 'We always looked forward to the times Adge was in town, and that week was no different,' says Philip. 'He would come in after they had set up at the club mid-evening, and we'd have a laugh and a sing-song. He might be there for an hour, an hour and a half, but he had a show to do, and he'd never have more than the odd pint. There were a couple of old boys he enjoyed talking to in the bar, but his band preferred to drink in the lounge. On that last night he spent about an hour with us, gave us a song, said his goodbyes and told us his next date in Hereford: "I'll make sure I see you all then."

'After the show he'd sometimes drop in for a late one if he saw the lights still on. He'd tap on the window, and Jacko would drag him in. That last night, he told us he wouldn't be back later, because he had to get home for an important meeting on the Sunday. We were used to show people dropping in. We were close to the big hotel in town, the Green Dragon, and a lot of the top acts at the Crystal Room stayed there. I remember Des O'Connor in with us, and I think he gave us a better show than the one he did at the Crystal Room. But Adge was different. Not showbizzy. He was just one of us.'

Back at the club he made contact with the owner, a colourful local entrepreneur called Des Macquire, and the manager Brian Turner. Tonight would be pay night, so there was plenty to talk about. When he started out on his career, with his modern-day Somerset folk songs, he never dreamed he'd be travelling the length and breadth of the land on the chicken-in-a-basket cabaret circuit, interspersing his beloved compositions with the odd Lionel Bart show tune, Country and Western numbers and even vintage rock. But the final encore was sacrosanct: the last song he would leave his audience with, that night as on all the other nights, would be *Drink Up Thy Zider*. At least the Crystal Room was not so far from home, and it was cosy and intimate compared with some of the soul-less great warehouses up North. For Hereford it was the only cabaret club in town, with its low ceiling and the glitter balls that gave it its name, and the stage mid-way along the room meant everyone was packed in tight and up close.

As the stars of the show, Adge and the Wurzels were supported by the comedy impressionist Jon Harvey and the compere and singer Cole Blacker, along with Chris Hawkins's three-piece house band. Adge had struck up a cheery relationship with the comedian – a twenty-two-year-old Lancashire lad who as Aiden J Harvey (another 'AJ') would enjoy success in the Eighties on London Weekend's *Copy Cats* – and they chatted happily together backstage. But they were all good guys, and by the end of the week everyone was satisfied that they had put on a decent little show, even if there was not too much eye-candy for the boys in the audience. A sophisticate from London might have looked askance at the club's moody black decor with wall paintings of Parisian life that smacked of the Fifties, but for young marrieds in Hereford in the mid-Seventies there was nowhere in town remotely like the Crystal Room. It even had a little dance floor where you could strut your disco stuff before the main act came on.

Those in closest contact with Adge that day have gone over their memories of it a thousand times, trying to make sense of it. None more so than John Tucker, who cannot get out of his mind a macabre turn in the coversation while they were out on their travels that morning. Seemingly out of the blue Adge said to him: 'You know, I've only been in two fights in my life. Both of them were in the school playground – and both the guys I fought with died in crashes.' John knew that only too well. One of them had been his close friend Leonard 'Ginger' Willcox, and even today he remembers the day his car left the road near Failand while on his way to meet mates in a late-night café in Bristol: October 1, 1961. The other had been more recent, in 1968, when Adge's good friend Adrian Raikes's brother Colin, better known as 'Buller', had died in his lorry near Bicester *en route* to pick up a load from the London Brick Company in Bedfordshire.

At first, John was baffled. What could have brought all this on? Then he remembered that the shiny white MGB in Adge's drive had only just come back from the menders after he had slewed it into a central reservation on the M4 near Swindon after a gig. He'd been travelling up to Hereford with the rest of the boys all week, so of course it would be great to get back in the driving seat. Better be careful, though. Joking aside, that crash had been a bit worrying. He'd only gone and fallen asleep at the wheel, hadn't he...?

A Distant Country Called Nailsea

Jack and Dorothy Cutler's son Alan John was born in a nursing home in Portishead, Somerset on November 19, 1931, half a dozen miles from the family's home on Nailsea High Street. The Whites, his mother's family, were a close, supportive bunch, and it made more sense for Dorothy to have her first child there, close to several female relatives, and leave her husband keeping business ticking over back at the shop. He certainly had plenty on his plate; since starting up with a taxi in Nailsea in 1924 he was in the process of expanding into coach hire, motorcycle and pushbike sales and even sweets and toffees, presumably to eat on the chara as it swept you away to far-off Weston or Burnham. 'Pride of Nailsea' was emblazoned on the front of the coaches, and that was the kind of place the village was, a proud and independent little island on the road to nowhere. Even today, with its thousands of Bristol commuter families, the most frequently asked question of the town is still: 'How exactly do you *get* there?'

Adge's brother Dave, his junior by some fourteen years and the youngest in a family that also included Roy and Rita, says: 'Father was the second person in Nailsea to own a car, after the village GP Dr Gornall. He worked in a garage business in Clifton, but he and his partner fell out over whether they should get a taxi service going in Nailsea. He asked his friend Charlie Goodenough how he thought one might go, Charlie said he thought it would do all right, so he took the plunge.'

Alan, his initials AJ converted to Adge at an early age, was not a strong child in his early years and to build him up, his mother dosed him with blood from butcher's meat and bread dipped in Oxo. Oxo with bread remained his favourite breakfast for the rest of his life. His first school was Christ Church School up to the age of eleven, and then he moved on to the Old Church School, usually known simply as Nailsea School, until it was time to start work at fourteen. Johnny Gower the headmaster and his wife Fanny, the assistant head, did not expect too much from the pupils they had mentally cast as future labourers and farm-hands, and in most ways Adge lived up to their low expectations. Needless to say, they came nowhere near to detecting his aptitude for language, both English and foreign, that would so entrance and impress people in the years to come.

For some time he sat next to George Enever, an evacuee from London, who recalled in 1993 that he was a good artist. Many who knew him in his younger days say the same, and his brother Dave and cousin Coreen Stone remember his drawings hanging on the wall of the living-cum-dining room behind the shop. Both of them talk of a pen-and-ink sketch of Gloucester Cathedral – 'I thought that was lovely,' says Dave – while another cousin, Rosalyn Wade, still has his detailed drawing of Princess Alexandra, a popular and glamorous young Royal of the Fifties. It is not work that would have sent the admissions committee of the Slade or Central St Martins into raptures, but yes, it is better than anything most of us could do, and some of his funny little cartoons in his later years were comfortably of professional standard. He told his wife Yvonne that the reason he was good at art was because he was booted out of music lessons for singing out of tune, so he had to spend his time drawing instead. It's a good Adge story.

Because of his skill with pen and ink it crossed Jack Cutler's mind that his son might make a good sign-writer, and for some time after school he took lessons in calligraphy. Nothing came of it professionally, but for the rest of his life he liked to impress friends with beautifully-crafted copper-plate letters. 'Your letter was very welcome and I treasure it for the writing and the way that it was written,' a jazzman friend from London wrote to him in 1960. Interestingly, when it came to sending business letters – like his string of appeals for work at folk clubs early in 1966 – he settled for a pleasant enough but unexceptional hand.

His speciality, as a workmate at Portishead B power station would later discover, was caricatures and head-and-shoulder portraits. 'He did a good painting of that policeman called Genge,' says Coreen, introducing us to one of the locals of old who constantly intrigued Adge, and Dave tells of 'a portrait in oils of an old boy who used to drink at the Star'. In 1955, more than a decade before they were briefly fellow Wurzels, Adge invited one of his Bristol jazz club friends and an accomplished professional artist, Brian Walker, along to the Nailsea Barbecue. 'Afterwards, old Adge took me back to his place to show me a staggering collection of his pastel drawings, mainly portraits,' he noted in his diary. 'Poetic, earthy directness, but a haunting, mesmeric sense of accurate characterization about them...'

Genge and the old boy at the Star were the kind of village characters Adge remembered and looked back on with affection all his life, and it must be said that Nailsea had its fair share of them. Back when he was growing up in the Thirties and Forties there were few distractions in small communities, and people *did* take more notice of their neighbours and see them as part of an on-going living tableau around them in a way that would be foreign to most of us today. Apart from which, before life had become ironed-out and homogenised by mass media, folk really were more idiosyncratic and quirky, and it was easy to pick up on their foibles. Adge loved all this, laughed at the nicknames they had acquired, and if they did not have one, would often enough come up with one of his own. In his late teens and twenties he would surround himself with mates who answered to the likes of Spanish Mayne and the Weston Poacher, while Dick Best's name was presumably amusing enough to need no further adornment. 'Spanish' was the late Cyril Mayne, in his younger days a talented electrician who designed the pioneering floodlights for Nailsea Town Football Club.

Those who really knew Adge swear that deep down he was a shy and reserved man, but one with a love for words and an urge to hide behind some mask or other and stand up and entertain people. His first public appearance can be traced back to around the eve of the Second World War. 'I gave my first performance when I was about seven, at Nailsea Village Institute,' he told the press when he was first breaking through. 'I sang *There'll Always Be A Nailsea*.' By this time, only the most optimistic of villagers were fooling themselves that Nailsea was too remote and insignificant to be troubled by the Luftwaffe. Most were well aware that Avonmouth and Bristol City Docks, Temple Meads and the aircraft works at Filton made them all too vulnerable to stray and jettisoned bombs, and the sight of the little lad standing up there piping his song of defiance must have brought a lump to many a throat. In fact the village got off lightly, but whenever there was action overhead the bar-room philosophers would be tuning into the various engine noises and sagely sorting out the Heinkels from the Hurricanes.

There'll always be a Nailsea from Coates's [sic] to West End
Where Station Road keeps winding
Down to Parsons Bend...

That's how Dave Cutler remembers it, though it could be that Adge came up with this version later, and merely sang a simpler variation of *There'll always be an England* back at the village institute. What Dave does know is that despite this early stage performance, his parents went through life seeing Adge as an introvert rather than a show-off. 'When you look at his career, I don't think my mother and father would have believed it of him,' he says. 'I remember when he was growing up a bit they'd been at a family party where they'd seen him clowning and making people laugh, and they just couldn't take in what they'd seen.'

Genge the policeman attracted so many stories that it is hard to know where fact ended and fiction began. Some remember baffling him by spotting his bike outside one pub and wheeling it down to the next one, while others swear he had little to do with pubs, except to steer well clear of them if trouble was brewing. 'We used to hang around in Adge's dad's garage, messing about and telling jokes,' Roy's best man Terry Elverd remembers. 'Sometimes Copper Genge would see us and duck in to while away a few minutes of his shift. "Shut that door," he'd say. "I don't want anyone spotting me in here." He wasn't one for looking for trouble. If there was fighting at the pub at West End, you can be sure he was somewhere on the other side of Coate's place.'

Adge used to tell of an exchange late one night that sounds suspiciously apocryphal:

Genge: Now then, young Cutler, what time do you call this? Adge: About half past midnight. Genge: Blimey, is it really? I must get home. The wife'll kill me.

Tales like these spread well beyond Nailsea. 'When Acker Bilk was at Weston Playhouse not long ago, he told stories about Copper Genge,' says Terry. 'He must have a special routine for West

Somerset, because he also came out with the one about the Paul Simon song *Trouble over Bridgwater*.' In fact Acker was no stranger to Nailsea back in the Fifties, after Adge had befriended him at his jazz club at the Crown and Dove in Bristol. The Cutlers had a piano, but when the Bristol jazz crowd came home with Adge for a late-night drink, Jack would turf them out into the big garage if they fancied a jam session. 'My parents used to rent a cottage from Jack Cutler, right next door to his shop and garage,' Richard Simmons recalls. 'Acker Bilk's band would sometimes practise in the garage, and when I was in bed as a little boy I'd drift off to sleep listening to the embryonic Paramount Jazz Band.' In fact these were not formal rehearsals, but just some of the guys enjoying themselves. Derek Paget, a jazz-loving neighbour some eight years younger than Adge, was another who found himself in on these sessions. 'I remember listening to them sitting on the wing of Roy's big American stock car,' he says, while admitting that his real reason for being round there was a fruitless pursuit of Rita Cutler.

On certain high days and holidays the garage would serve as a makeshift showcase for the televison sets sold by a neighbouring electrical shop, with a number of them dispersed around the room, their nine-inch and twelve-inch screens aglow. It's reckoned that most of the male population of the village was gathered there to see Arsenal beat Liverpool in the 1950 Cup Final – 'Lewis got 'em both', a remarkable number of old-timers still remember – while many families saw TV for the first time when the garage opened its oily doors for the Coronation in 1953.

Adge's life in Bristol would impinge on the happy home in other ways than the occasional visit by Acker's boys. 'He was always out trying new things,' Terry Elverd remembers. 'One night he had the bright idea of drinking cheap red wine and cider – "Red Biddy" – in the Red Lion on Blackboy Hill. "Alan came home in a hell of a state last night," Mrs Cutler told me the next day. "The goldfish was dead on the carpet, he'd drunk the contents of the bowl...'" before going on to make his mark on the house in other ways with which we need not concern ourselves here.

Other village notables included one 'Ambone and Arthur 'Lightning' Windsor, who had had a drop one day and was tottering along the High Street when he met posh Vicar Powell.

'Drunk again, Windsor?' 'Aye, so am I, Vicar.'

Terry Elverd says Lightning lived a hundred yards down the road from the Queen's Head, but he was in the pub so often that you would hardly know it. One Sunday his wife was so fed up with waiting for him to come home for his dinner that she went along and slammed it down on the bar. Lightning didn't turn a hair, but probably made a mental note to tell her off for not bringing the salt and pepper.

Farmer Header Brock was so called because the first thing he did when he was given a pint was blow the froth off, Terry remembers. In the Star at Tickenham one night they were discussing the looming onset of decimalisation. 'Nah,' Header proclaimed, 'they might go along with it in Bristol, but it'll never catch on around here.'

Walt Harrall, the rag-and-bone man, was another familiar sight with his whippet dog. On one of the Royal Oak recordings Adge can be heard introducing him as 'the Easton-in-Gordano ambassador'. Walt's brother, who lived in the old jail, was universally known as Dog for the very good reason that he looked like a spaniel. They didn't mince words in Nailsea in those days. Another face who stood out from the crowd was 'an old feller called Ernie, pretty well a tramp but not quite', while Stan, the barber from the North, was such a comic turn that the kids would go around for a haircut on Saturday mornings even if they didn't need one. Some of the nicknames were short and to the point. Another barber, a basin cut specialist, was Palmer, who shared his name with a big toffee company so was forever Chewy. Since one of the makers' top brands was Camp Toffee, maybe he got off lightly.

Then there was the Dan'l Windle drama, Dan'l being one of those old chaps who used to 'black cat' one another in pubs, as in 'My cat's blacker'n yours.' 'No t'aint.' The telling of tall stories is a time-honoured tradition in the countryside, so Adge didn't really think too much about it when he happily sang:

> *Hark at 'ee, Jacko,*
> *true as it can be,*
> *Ol' Dan'l Windle told I,*
> *An' 'e's a bigger liar 'n thee.*

There were those who cared about Dan'l Windle who did mind, however, and some stiff letters were exchanged before the fuss died down.

And then there was one of the best-remembered characters of all, George Rollings, whose version of how *Drink Up Thy Zider* came to be thought up, if not written, is generally taken to be probable. The scene was the Black Horse at Clapton-in-Gordano and George's memories were recorded on tape by the broadcaster Mel Gordon, working for local radio. Sadly, neither is still with us. 'We were in there one night and we had this barrel of cider,' George told Mel. 'We were singing all sorts of rubbish, and this was how *Drink Up Thy Zider* was born in there, 'cos one would say sommat, and t'other would say sommat else, and somebody said "Drink up thee cider, George" and then somebody said "And pass us round the jar." And then it went like: "Drink up thee cider, George, thee bissn't goin' far..." Adge cottoned on to that and said oh, we could sing that, so we added a little bit more to it and he took it home with him an' made it into what it is. The next thing we knew he made a record and that was on it. But yes, I was the George of the cider.'

A very potent reason why Adge clung on to his memories of the Nailsea of old lay in the vast changes he saw in the community during his comparatively short life. In the census of 1931, the year he was born, the population was just over two thousand – five hundred fewer than when mining and glass making had flourished there in the mid-Nineteenth century. In 1974 it stood at around fourteen thousand, and today it is some seventeen thousand, with no significant further expansion planned. Most of the houses went up in the Sixties and early Seventies in what for the locals was a baffling spate of frenzied activity, and there was much concern that facilities and infrastructure were failing to keep pace with the booming population; this, after all, was not a designated New Town, with Government funding and strategic planning behind it. As we have hinted, Adge grew to love Guernica, in Basque Spain. 'He used to say it was just like Nailsea before it was spoiled,' Dave Cutler says, and since its name is now synonymous with the devastation of modern warfare because of Picasso's great masterpiece, we must conclude that Spain's post-war rebuilding was a good deal more successful than Britain's attempts at town planning in the Sixties.

Was the young Adge musical? Dave laughs at the suggestion: 'He tried desperately hard to be, but he never got anywhere. I remember him trying to play the trombone. He got nowhere, but it wasn't for want of trying. This was when he first came out of the Army, and had nothing very much to do. He never played our parents' piano. Roy played it a little bit, and so did Rita, but not Adge. Adge went through life unable to read or write a note of music. My Uncle Bill used to play the accordion, and my father's other brother played the spoons at family get-togethers, but that was about it.

Ah yes, Bill Cutler. Terry Elverd's wife Barbara's family used to run the Bird in Hand pub in Nailsea, and if they saw Adge's Uncle Bill heading in their direction, her father would close and lock the piano lid.

So he wasn't a great player, then?

'Remember Les Dawson?' says Barbara.

But loving music and letting it engulf him in happiness, that was something that was becoming increasingly a part of Adge's life, as his cousin Rosalyn Wade remembers. 'It was in the living room at the back of the cycle shop,' she says. 'I was visiting one day with my mother and all the family were there – Uncle Jack and Auntie Dor plus Alan, Roy, Rita and Dave. The radio was playing and when *Twelfth Street Rag* came on, Alan decided he would dance me round the room, even though he was twenty and I was about five. So there we were, with him twirling me round the room, my legs waving everywhere. They were all shouting "Alan, put her down, she's only a little girl", but he wouldn't until the tune had finished. That tune still comes on the radio sometimes, and when it does I always think of that unexpected dancing lesson from Alan.'

His cousin Coreen Stone also remembers him as a bit of a card: 'My mum was having tea at our gran's cottage at Clapton-in-Gordano one day when Adge picked up a big lump of cheese and made these great teeth marks in it, just for fun. The assembled company was not amused. But I remember him best at Nailsea, in the bike shop, when our gran was living with them towards the end of her life. It was a tight squeeze at that time with my aunt and uncle, the four children and my gran living there, and the outside loo down the lane beside the house. They weren't on mains sewers. As a family they must have been better off than a lot in Nailsea, but they weren't living in luxury.

'They had a caravan in Cornwall where they went on holiday with the two younger children, Rita and David, and when I was in my early teens I would go to stay with gran to keep her company. Adge and Roy were there, but they were out at work all day, and when they came home they were big grown men who didn't have much to do with me. Adge drank red wine with his meal and I do remember that because not many people in Nailsea did. I have a feeling he brought chaps back to play instruments one night, but of course I had nothing to do with that. What he did include me in one year was his float at Nailsea Flower Show, when he and his friends paraded around with a barrel of cider. I went with Rita, who was a year older than me.' Adge's neighbour Derek Paget still has a photograph of this, with the float got up like a boat – the *Scrump* – and Adge with his trombone. 'He played the trombone then,' Derek explains. Well, up to a point, Lord Copper, but he was doubtless capable of making silly noises with it to attract the crowd's attention.

Although Adge was clueless as a mechanic, with a family like his he was surrounded by exciting wheels, and it was a passion that stayed with him all his life. Before he could ride a motorbike he was a keen cyclist, and had fun running the Nailsea Hawks pushbike dirt track team on a muddy track on a field his father owned. In fact the Cutler boys' contacts must have been good for business in various ways. 'I went to school with Roy, and he tipped us off when nice new bikes came into the shop,' one old friend says. 'I bought one off his dad for £5 and seemed to take years paying it off at half a crown a time.'

When Adge turned sixteen he became one of the first owners of a new post-war BSA 350 – his father was a BSA stockist – and it was on this in Bristol that he suffered an accident that would follow him right through to the post-mortem report after his final crash: 'The second toe is missing from the right foot, having been previously amputated, and so also is the tip of the great toe on the right side'. Roy Cutler, four years younger than Adge, still remembers it well: 'He came off that BSA in my brand new pair of wellington boots! There was no damage to the bike except maybe a bent foot-rest. We were always falling off motorbikes, but Adge was unlucky that time. My father and mother were at the pictures at the Curzon in Clevedon and after PC Genge had come round to tell us about the accident, I phoned the cinema and a message was flashed on the screen.' Roy went on to be a far more proficient rider than Adge, winning the Army's coronation motorcycle trials in Cyprus in 1953, and later becoming locally known for his stock car racing exploits at the Bristol speedway stadium at Knowle.

Ted Cowell, who years later would play a significant part in Adge's life, recalls first meeting him at what was then a cider house called the Quinton in Park Place, Clifton in 1951-52. 'I was studying architecture in Bristol and it was one of our favourite pubs, but as well as students you would get one or two bikers in there. We got on very well with them, and one of them was Adge, who came along with his mate Spanish Mayne. He told me he was writing songs, and I'm pretty sure one of them was *Drink Up Thy Zider*.' If that is true, it dates its composition to half a dozen years earlier than is usually supposed.

Jack Cutler would run coach trips to both the speedway and stock cars at Knowle, as well as to Wembley for football internationals. This was in conjunction with the Queen's Head pub, which organised a savings club to spread the cost over the year. Adge would go on some of these weekends away, even though he was no great soccer fan, and what he lacked in excitement at the game he more than made up for in enjoyment before and after it. He would forever tell variations of a story about one of the travellers who forgot where the coach was parked and told a stranger who was trying to help him that it had been 'on the Nailsea side of London'. Then, according to Terry Elverd, there was the time Header Brock lost his mates in the big crowd outside Wembley Stadium and asked a policeman if he had seen any Nailsea blokes around. 'What do they look like?' the copper asked, deadpan.

John Tucker reckons Adge himself was just as much a source of fun as Header Brock ever was. 'There were about forty of us in this hotel foyer, and there was an Irish girl hovering around. In the end she went over to Adge and said excuse me, can you tell me what nationality you are? "Nailsea." That was so typical. He was full of odd little words and phrases that made you laugh. I was with him at the Salthouse in Clevedon one night when he ordered a pork pie. "Mustard?" "No, I'll have it neat."'

One of Adge's teenage enthusiasms, incongruously, was the Army Cadets, and although there was a corps in Nailsea, for some reason he was attached to the one at Sixways, Clevedon. 'That's where I got to know him,' says Haydn James, who still lives in the town. 'I knew his mum and dad, too – they were nice people – and I'd drop in for a cup of tea when I was in Nailsea. Adge wasn't the greatest Army cadet, but he was all right. Best of all, he was a good laugh, and he'd always be right there in the sing-songs when we went off to camp. We used to go to Lulworth Cove, at an old wartime camp, and on days off we would go to Weymouth. I still have a picture of us there. Really, it's just a picture of a group of lads standing together and laughing, but Adge had the bright idea of putting a cap on the pavement in front of us, to look as if we were busking, and he's holding a kazoo, one of those tin things you blow into and it makes the sound you get with a comb and paper. That's all he could play, mind. We had a band that won cups, but he wasn't in it with his kazoo! When I was called up, having been in the Cadets was useful for me, on the gunnery side; you knew what you had to do, you knew what you were in for. I'm not sure how useful Adge found it in the Pay Corps.'

A close friend in the couple of years before Adge was called up in 1949 was Bernard Petteford, who had come to Nailsea in 1947 when his father had started a coal business there. 'When we first arrived our house was in the High Street, and that's when I met Adge, with his father's shop close by. He'd only recently had his motorbike accident, but he was getting back on his feet, and we took to going to St John's Hall at the bottom of Blackboy Hill in Bristol [now part of the auctioneers Dreweatt Neate's salerooms in Apsley Road] to learn how to ballroom dance, though "stumble" would be a better word. Then I joined the Royal Marines with a view to making a career of it, and my first posting was on the aircraft carrier HMS *Vengeance*. On my first leave, Adge was home from National Service, and we went to a dance at the Winter Gardens in Weston-super-Mare. One way and another we missed the last bus, and when Adge rang his father for a lift, he didn't want to know. We ended up sharing a bed in a B&B above a shop, and the next morning he woke early because he had to get back to Bulford Barracks on Salisbury Plain. He went downstairs, couldn't find anybody to let him out, and complained that there were "all these cats at the bottom of the stairs" that were also wanting a quick exit. By then it was clear that he was going to be late reporting for duty, so I rang the barracks and spoke to a bloke. "You bloody tell him to get back here fast," he said.'

At one time Bernard and Adge were going out with two sisters,

'Cecilia for me and Pearl for Adge. Pearl later told me that when they went to the pictures one night at the Rex in Bedminster, she gave him a ten shilling note and never saw the change. Later, when I married my first wife, Adge was my best man. The reception was in a café on the Wells Road at Knowle, and he gave a funny speech that made them laugh. To be honest, it's not a day I like to think about very much. His mother gave me a warning when she heard of my wedding plans. "Marry in haste and repent at leisure," she said, and she was so right. Happily, I got it right second time around.

'After that, with me married, Adge and I seemed to drift apart. I could never get the relationship back. I never thought he'd be an entertainer, but he certainly was, and he wrote some very funny songs. He wasn't over-handsome but as far as the girls were concerned he had a way with him, with his grin and that odd little laugh. And he'd been a good pal to me, with no side to him.'

In 1954 Bernard's father fell ill and he left the Marines to run the family business. He branched out into transport and when his wife Ruth bought him a Christmas present of a hot air balloon flight, he realised that this was an exciting medium through which to advertise his coal business, which had expanded to take in Bath, Bristol and Weston-super-Mare. He got his pilot's licence and bought his first balloon in 1980 from Don Cameron, since when the couple have travelled the world on flying holidays and at one time ran flights in craft carrying up to sixteen people. Like Adge as a local boy made good, Bernard had no wish to leave Nailsea and still lives there; but their careers took very different routes, and it is not hard to see how their paths diverged as they grew up.

Since leaving school, Adge's working life had been as low-grade as his teachers had predicted: hanging around serving in his father's bike shop, a labourer in a market garden, the statutory spell at the big cider company founded in Nailsea by Redvers Coate in 1924, the year Jack Cutler started his taxi company. Adge worked in the warehouse, humping huge loads of apples around, the side of cider that made a man anything but merry be. In truth, whisper it not, he never was all *that* fond of it as the years went by, just as soon drinking beer or red wine. Ted Cowell laughs about it, now: 'There'd be these country shows when some old farmer would plonk a cask of cider on the stage and say "Here y'are, Adge, here's a drop of the good stuff," and half the time he used to pass it on to me!'

Dave Cutler says he did not really know his big brother until after he had finished his National Service. 'He didn't like the Army at all, it was obviously too restricted and regimented for him,' he says. 'Why did he join the Cadets? I think the idea was probably all right until he actually *did* it. My other brother Roy liked the Army, went abroad and was big in motorcycling. But it wasn't for Adge.' Roy remembers when Adge was detailed to take a case full of money from the Pay Corps in Devizes to Norton Fitzwarren, near Taunton, and ended up in Cornwall after falling asleep on the train. It is a story that foreshadowed several hapless adventures with the band's pay when he took the job as Acker Bilk's road manager. But there were a few shovels to be wielded, ditches to be delved and ditties to be composed before he embarked on that crazy period of his life.

I Was on the Chippings, Boy

Lyric poets notoriously blossom early and die young, and though Adge was no Keats, Shelley or Byron, it is a fact – perhaps a painful fact – that all his most creative writing was done when he was in his early to middle twenties – the time in the Fifties when he was spending his Tuesday and Saturday nights lapping up the atmosphere at the jazz clubs at the Crown and Dove, and spending long days working as a labourer on or around the emerging Portishead B power station.

In his younger days, the late poet laureate Ted Hughes – a close contemporary of Adge, though there the comparisons end – was a great believer in creative men earning their living through hard and mentally undemanding physical work, though even he squirmed when he was down a hole in Cambridge one morning and his old tutor greeted him with a completely matter-of-fact 'Good morning, Mr Hughes'.

At least Adge did not run the risk of that kind of embarrassment, but rightly or wrongly, neither did he feel he had any choice other than labouring when he came home after national service in 1951. By far the most reliable source of decently-paid manual work locally was Portishead B, started in 1949 but still a comforting several years away from completion, and once on board he soon began to feel at home there.

Admittedly, back in Nailsea at weekends, he privately joked about some of his workmates – 'He was always telling us funny stories about the Paddies he worked with,' his old pal Terry Elverd recalls – but he was happy and relaxed in their company, and found them a supportive and receptive audience to his quips and 'ditties'.

Apart from which, some of them were quite bright enough to keep him on his toes.

He was famously daft and subversive, with funny little phrases forever on his lips, and the lads on the site were not the first or last to pick up on his habit of scribbling notes on the back or inside slider of Woodbine packets. What also came through again were his talent as an artist – and his eye for the main chance.

'In about 1955 Adge and I were working on Portishead B for the civil engineers Charles Brand,' Keith Gissing remembers. 'Our job was to rub down the joints on a concrete retaining wall, boring work that seemed never-ending. We were visited once or twice a day by a senior supervisor called Les Cobb, who never spoke but just glared at us from under his peaked cap. He wore a duffel coat with pockets deep enough for his arms to go right up to his elbows. I had no idea how artistic Adge was until he found a yellow crayon and drew a very life-like but unflattering caricature of Cobb on the by now pristine wall. We didn't hang around to see the reaction; we jacked before we could be sacked!'

A particular chum was Hector Hamer, then of Portishead and now living just along the coast at Redcliff Bay, who worked with Adge building the new railway station that was part of the power station project. The old GWR station was demolished in 1954 to ease access to Portishead B, and a modern terminus was built about a quarter of a mile nearer town. It lasted for just ten years as a passenger station before falling to the Beeching axe in September 1964, and much to the grief of present-day rail campaigners, a Waitrose petrol station now stands on its site.

'I went to sea as a radio officer, but got tired of sitting in a little cabin all day and wanted a bit of action and a social life,' says Hector, who was older than Adge by eighteen months. 'I left the Marconi company, went to the Labour Exchange in Portishead and got a docket to go down to where Charles Brand were building the new railway station. That's where I met Adge, one of twenty of us lined up on a level stretch of ashes with picks and shovels, digging the drainage trench from there to the foundations of the platform. He was a character right from the word go, a workmate who would always see the funny side of things.

'His job would be primarily on the cement mixer, with its big gauge box, a winch to tip in the contents and a chain to feed in the right amount of water. Ten to twelve of us would be coming and going with wheelbarrows, all day long, and this is where Adge and I would meet and chat together. On wet days when we couldn't work there was Mr Hoddinott's tea cabin across the way. That was always good. We'd bury our super-shiny shovels in the sand – we each had our own, treasured them and kept them gleaming like chromium – and settle down in Hoddinott's for big bacon sandwiches and cups of tea.

'Adge would get the back of a fag packet, open it out on to the blank side and start scribbling. At first we had no idea what he was doing – a shopping list, racing tips? – but it soon became clear. "Hey, Hec," he said to me one day. "What rhymes with Bristol Docks?" I thought about the time I was on a Donaldson boat, Avonmouth to Montreal, and we'd go down the Bristol Channel and then round the corner past Swansea...

'"Mumbles Rocks?"

'And that rhyme found its way into *I'm the Captain of a Dredger*.'

Hector says that as time went by, he discovered that Adge would be trying out all these numbers in pubs, like *Pill, Pill* at the Duke of Cornwall down there on a Saturday night. It could be, however, that he made a more significant contribution to his friend's future than by giving him a rhyme for 'Docks'. A hero of *Children's Hour* on the radio was Wurzel Gummidge, a scruffy rustic scarecrow who came to life, and being a city slicker from metropolitan Portishead, Hector would sometimes joke with Adge about his slow, country manner and call him 'Wurzel'. 'Wurzel', Adge would repeat with that chuckle of his, rolling the word around in his mouth, all urrs and arrs. 'You don't know, do you?' says Hector. 'But I like to think that when he came to naming that first little group of his, he thought of that.'

One wet day the two of them wandered out to the cement shelter on the building site. There was a great pile of brown paper Ferrocrete cement bags lying around, and Adge had the bright idea of dressing up in them: 'He cut the end off some of the bags with his pocket knife and we made ourselves a pair of leggings held up with binder cord, another pair to make the lower part, one on each arm and then another over our bodies, with a hole in the top for the head and two on the sides for our arms. Then he made a great triangular paper hat, and when he got out in the rain, dancing around in all this gear, the lads in Hoddinott's saw him and fell about laughing.

'We were together there for a few months and the job was going quite well when I met my downfall. Working down that trench was thirsty work, so after I'd been home for dinner I'd pop into the Anchor on the way back and get a couple of flagons of cider. One of the pipelayers liked a drop, and kept a flagon in a glazed pipe, but one of the foremen got wind of it and said to me "No more cider on the job, or you're up the road."

'I said "Well, I like my cider, Bert, I'm not going to give it up," so he said "In that case, up the road Friday." So that was me back to sea! The last time I saw Adge at around that time was when I was home on leave and he said "Hey, Hec, we're all going up to that Trawsfynydd atomic station in North Wales. Come up with us. The craic will be something marvellous up there." But by this time I was feeling at home at sea again, and I told him that though I'd love to go up there with him and the lads, it wasn't going to happen.'

A workmate already known to Adge was Haydn James, a friend from his unlikely stint as an Army Cadet, and he remembers that in among all the clowning there was seriously tough work to be done: 'At one time we were pulling down all the granaries on the dockside, with dust and grain everywhere. It was pretty hard going but we were young, we could do it. There were always laughs and jokes with him, but you wouldn't necessarily have known he'd go on to do what he did.'

Another graphic account of life building Portishead B, at this time for the Mitchell engineering group, came some years ago when the local radio presenter Mel Gordon interviewed George Rollings, who, as we note elsewhere, played a significant cameo role in the Adge Cutler story. 'Out on the bay, on the job, he was known as Jacko,' George recalled. 'Everybody called him Jacko, and they'd shout at him "More rods, Jacko, more rods." "Jacko here, Jacko there, Jacko every bloody where," he'd be singing. It was about then that he started writing songs. He must have gone home and carried them in his head and then worked on them.

'If he went into the Black Horse in Clapton-in-Gordano, he'd strike up with [the Harry Champion music hall song] *The End of My Old Cigar* and sing it to anyone who was listening, whether they knew him or not. Soon after that, they would be songs of his own.' The Fifties were the time of calypso music, with the first wave of immigrants from the West Indies making their mark and the great Windies trio of Walcott, Worrall and Weekes blossoming into world stars. The under chargehand at Mitchell's was Mr Edwards. The man in charge of the whole site was Mr Dickinson.

'We were stood there one day and Cutler said "Here, wass think o' this?" and he sang:

'At Mitchell's we have bags of fun
With Bill Edwards and Dickinson.

'I'm sure he could have gone on, but everybody gave him a clap and that was the end of it.'

Another song that owes everything to Portishead B is *The Mixer Man's Lament*, with its lines:

I was on the chippings, boy, Paddy on the sand,
Weasel on the mixer, we made a happy band.

'I remember Weasel,' George Rollings told Mel Gordon. 'When we put the jetty out for Albright and Wilson's [then owners of a large chemical plant at Avonmouth], he used to drive they mixers, with the sand and the chippings going in, and all the dust. At weekend he'd be inside it chipping away at the concrete so it was clean and ready for Monday. He was in there one day and they started the mixer up, and there he was in there. When he got out he hurled his shovel as far as he could and Adge said that's right, Weasel, chuck thee shovel in there and jack it [walk off the job] like a man.'

Weasel was Arthur Holder of Glebe Avenue, Portishead, a dozen years older than Adge, so in his mid-thirties when he was immortalised in song. George Rollings said he was called Weasel because he looked like a Weasel. Weasel claimed he was called Weasel by his pals when he was about five, because he 'could shin up a tree faster than anyone else... and I could swim when I was seven'. If climbing trees and adept swimming are what most people think of when they think of weasels, then the late Mr Holder was doubtless to be believed. Others might feel the late Mr Rollings had a point...

Arthur Holder was tracked down to the Anchor at Portishead by a *Western Daily Press* reporter, Ray Wood, in November 1967, a few days after his protegé George Lefeuvre won the World Cider Drinking Championships; more about that seemly evening elsewhere in this book. His youngest boon companion, eighteen-year-old Andy McCarthy, told the journalist: 'When Weasel was working at the docks, if anyone dropped anything in the water, he would be in there and got it...'

'That's right,' smiled Weasel, 'I could even find a penny.'

This kind of ridiculous bragging brightened many a long day for Adge and some of the more savvy men on site, along with the endless boasts about prodigious drinking feats. Weasel told Ray Wood that his regular daily intake, 'if the atmosphere was right', would be eighteen or nineteen pints, yet at the grand championships he had shocked and horrified his backers by downing just four in an hour. Apparently it was 'too cold' that night.

George Rollings told Mel Gordon of a slapstick moment that could have come straight out of the Keystone Cops, by no means the only incident in which Adge is made to sound like some hapless silent movie comic. 'Some old boy from Portishead come along with the tea on the back of a low trailer for one of us to take round, and one day I said to Cutler "You better come along with I. Just sit on the trailer, fill up the cups and give 'em to the blokes." We went out to what we called the back hills, right the way down to the sea, and we were goin' down this slope, steeper than Clapton 'ill, creeping along at less than five miles an hour, and would you believe it, the back wheel come off. Cutler shot straight out over the road, down the bank and on to the rocks, right by the sea. Could've been killed, couldn't he? Cutler said "I ain't comin' on that bloody job no more."

'Adge was a nice bloke, a very nice bloke, but he was a clever bloke. At Portishead, old Jack Patterson, he was the general foreman, he put me in charge of the tractors and fuel, and I had to go down to the Clock Garage every other day to fill up this forty-gallon drum of petrol. Cutler came up and he said to I, I tell you what, he said, you fix me up with a drop of petrol, I'll pick you up and take you to work and I'll take you home. Oh, I said, that's no problem. I got this Esso can and gave him two gallons, sommat like that, poured it in the car, and home we went.

'The next morning I was waiting for him and this little Morgan sports pulled up, right down low on the ground – he had four wheels, not three – with a canvas roof and they bucket seats with canvas in. He said get in, we'm late, and after a struggle I got in and me head was like a molehill sticking up into the roof. When we started that canvas started flapping on me head. "Cor blimey Cutler," I said, and we got a stick to hold it up above me head... When we got to work, I and Cutler, he picked up the foot pump and I said "What's to do wi' 'ee, then?" He said "I put 'im under the front wheel because I haven't got a handbrake."'

Later there was the famous pick-up from the Triangle in Clevedon every morning, when ten of Adge's workmates would pile into his Bedford Dormobile and pay ten shillings a week each for the return trip to Portishead B. A mate of George Rollings, Les, was one customer. George Dimond, a painter and decorator, was another. 'He'd drive us to work tapping the steering wheel and singing these songs,' he remembers. 'I was decorating at Portishead power station when Adge was there working for Mitchell's, and we'd meet up in breaks and he'd always be playing around with these ditties – we called them ditties – in his head.'

'He were a businessman,' George Rollings recalled in his recording for Mel Gordon. 'He was thinking all the time. I said to my missus, he were the type of bloke, with his way with words, he could have sat down and wrote a symphony. It might've taken him a long time, but he'd have done it. I never heard him swear (sic) and I never seen him lose his temper. As a mate he was very good. Mind you, he wasn't very fast coming forward in the pub to buy you a pint.' Inevitably, the thirsty work on site paved the way for a strong drinking culture, and Adge was by no means immune to it. Throughout this book we encounter friends and acquaintances' impressions of his attitude to alcohol – his intake was modest, say some, it was anything but modest, according to others. The truth lies in the fact that he was by no means an alcoholic and that to some people, the strains of *Drink Up Thy Zider* ringing in their ears, he was remarkably abstemious. But make no mistake, Adge Cutler could put it back, and there were plenty of workmates at Portishead B who were happy to join him.

'He'd get paid on a Thursday, go to the White Lion on the way home and go for a sub on Friday,' his brother Dave recalls. And his friend Terry Elverd remembers being told a quite remarkable story by Adge's mother, after his gang had been rained off at the power station: 'She said he went home via the Albion in Portishead, crashed out in bed and came down at about six o'clock in the evening, asking where his breakfast was. She duly cooked him bacon and eggs and he went off in his minibus to pick up the other guys for the morning shift. I suppose that's a bit of a laugh, thinking six in the evening was six in the morning, but it's a bit disturbing, too, isn't it? Like a lot of funny people, Adge had his dark side.'

There was nobody to make breakfast for him, morning or evening, when he moved to North Wales in the late Fifties, tempted by talk of the big money to be made building the new atomic power station at Trawsfynydd. It was a miserable, chilly existence living in a shanty town in the depths of deepest grey slate country forever lashed by rain, far from his mates and the Bristol jazz scene that had become a pivotal part of his life. He suffered creatively, too, with no evidence of any significant songwriting at this stage of his life; when it came to making music out of double-barrelled place names, it seems Stanton Drew and Chew Magna had more potential than Blaenau Ffestiniog. His old mate Mr Acker Bilk was suddenly making it big when Britain woke up to trad jazz, or at least an easily digestible version of it. In January 1960 *Summer Set* entered the charts. With a title like that, no wonder Adge thought he was being called home.

Roadie to Acker, Road to Spain

As the Fifties wore on, the (now demolished) Crown and Dove in Rupert Street, Bristol was turning into an increasingly important port of call for Adge and his mates Spanish Mayne, the Weston Poacher and Dick Best. Close to the Bridewell and the fire station, it was a tough and scruffy city pub, but for jazz fans on Tuesday and Saturday nights its upstairs room took on a magic all its own, with live sessions by bands and players who would go on to make their mark far beyond the West Country. On stage on Tuesdays were Acker Bilk from Pensford with his Paramount Jazz Band, who already had quite a following, while on Saturdays the spotlight was on a young bunch from Bristol, the Cassey Bottom Jazz Band.

A member of the Casseys was Keith Box, who along with his future wife Geraldine was very much one of the Crown and Dove in-crowd. 'Keith and I met Adge there on the Saturday nights, with the Cassey Bottom – later the Oriole –Jazz Band,' says Geraldine. 'We would have been sixteen or so, he about twenty-three. That's where he first met Johnny Macey, who was part of the original Wurzels.' It seems that even in town Adge did not leave his Nailsea roots far behind, as the Boxes still have clear memories of his tales of Copper Genge and other members of the village's all-star cast.

Adge made a big step forward when he went along to one of the Tuesday sessions with a pal from home, Terry Elverd. 'He was going to the Crown and Dove trad nights before I was,' Terry remembers. 'But he knew I was a fan, so one day he said "Come and hear this guy on clarinet, he's marvellous." So we went along, and of course it was Acker, and would you believe it, I already knew him. I was an apprentice at the Alma Garage in Feeder Road, and he used to work for a machinery firm called Cox's. I went over and said hello Acker, I didn't know you could play clarinet. "Oh yes," he said, "I picked it up in the Army." Of course when I got back to Adge he wanted to know what it was all about, so I told him. He couldn't believe anybody he knew could actually be on speaking terms with a man like that. I said tell me what you want to hear, and I'll ask him to play it for you. He named a song, I can't remember what, I said hey, Acker, can you play this for a mate of mine, and that was it.

'Adge and Acker were buddies from that day on.'

It was at the Crown and Dove that Adge first stood up and sang his songs anywhere other than in homely Nailsea or Pill or the pubs in between them. On Tuesdays he would very often perform unaccompanied while Acker and his boys took tea, or whatever, but the Cassy Bottom crew, or at least some of them, were happy to busk along behind him. 'Of course, he couldn't read music, and brought no band parts along with him,' says Keith Box, a clarinet wizard good enough to go on to play with the Ken Colyer band. 'It was no use asking him what key we'd be doing a song in, but we'd hit B-flat and see where he went from there. In fairness, once he started singing, he kept the tune and key pretty well.

'He used to drive us to London for work and it was a worry, he was always dropping off to sleep. We had to keep poking him to wake him up. In fact he himself was worried about dropping off, and told us how he'd woken up at the wheel once and discovered he was nearly home.' These scares aside, Keith invariably enjoyed Adge's company, while his mates could also be good value: 'Dick Best was living in Hanham at this stage. I was on the bus there when he dropped off the platform when it was passing the Blue Bowl, ran across the road and didn't break his stride as the pub door opened in front of him. You could have rehearsed it a hundred times for a film and not got it so perfect. The Oriole band ran a second jazz evening in Pill on Sunday nights with another Wurzel-to-be, Reg Quantrill, and again Adge would stand up and sing. 'I sat on the door taking the money, often with Keith's mum and dad,' says Geraldine. 'People queued to pay us one and three (around 6p) to get in – and then it folded, and I had all this money. Reg said "Oh, go on, you just spend it," so I bought my wedding cake with it!'

Derek Paget was another member of the Crown and Dove crowd: 'I worked at Maggs' department store in Clifton, and some Tuesdays I'd stay on in town and get a lift back with Adge at the end of the evening. At the Crown and Dove we saw ourselves as very different from the Avon Cities crowd, more wild and free. There were certainly some characters. On Tuesday nights somebody we called Nature Boy used to sit on a sill behind Acker's band wearing only a singlet and shorts at all times of year. It would be there where, in the very early Sixties, Adge would stand and sing his songs. He was well liked, and they went down well. I think early black folk music was among his influences somewhere. I certainly admired his ability to come up with tuneful melodies that were all his own. As for the words, he was forever scribbling on the back of Woodbines packets.' Another of his Bristol haunts was the Ship on Redcliff Hill, where he sang backed by the Stainer Collett Seven, in which Acker Bilk's sometime trumpeter John Stainer and Dave Collett on piano played alongside Reg Quantrill on guitar.

Adge's crew were known as the Nailsea Ravers, noted for their appreciation of the music with raucous shouts of 'Whang, you buggers, whang,' interspersed occasionally by 'Gi' 'em cowcake!'

and 'Milk the buggers, they'm in pain!' This was decidedly not what happened with the Avon Cities crowd. 'Shout "Whang!" there and it would be like shouting "Bollocks!" in St Paul's Cathedral,' Adge confided to his friend Brian Walker.

By around 1960 – maybe eight years after he first began going to the Crown and Dove – he was indeed well known and popular. One of the crowd, Norman Lott, recalls a gang of them going over to Nailsea for his birthday party at a pub. 'The bit I remember most was at the end of the evening, just as everyone was leaving,' he muses. 'Adge finished his drink and then threw the empty glass and smashed it against the wall. I never knew why he did that.' Kathy Shortman was another Crown and Dove jazz fan who enjoyed Adge's company: 'We went with him to parties and festivals, and when he went on tour with Acker, he sent me postcards. I wish I'd kept them; I can't remember what they said, but I do remember his beautiful copper-plate handwriting.'

The time Adge was becoming a face in Bristol coincided exactly with Acker Bilk's overnight success as a trad jazz icon after a decade or more on the road, years when Tuesday night at the Crown had been a comfortingly regular source of income. Like Adge when he had first heard that magic clarinet, nobody in Britain had ever quite encountered anything like *Summer Set,* which was released on the eve of the Sixties; after it entered the charts in January 1960 it stayed there for nineteen weeks, peaking at number five. All of a sudden the Bilk bandwagon was rolling everywhere, and he needed people around him – people who would do the donkey work, but also good old Somerset boys who would speak his language and keep him grounded. Enter you-know-who.

'Adge was with me as a roadie for four years, driving, setting up the gear and doing all the usual kind of things roadies do,' Acker says today. ' He was a good lad. As a roadie he was rotten, but there was never a dull moment with him, and we had a lot of fun. Well, perhaps "rotten" is too strong a word, but he kept forgetting things, and he was not the most efficient roadie I've ever had. He was the funniest, though, and there were always daft things happening – just little things, but we'd be falling about laughing when he told us about them afterwards.

'One night we were playing at the Salthouse in Clevedon, so he was pretty well on home territory. He was with us as we were playing at one end of this packed room, when he saw a bloke beckoning to him furiously at the very far end. Adge was a mate of this feller, saw him every week, but the way he was urging him to come over made him think it must be something really important. So off he goes, fighting his way through the fag smoke and all these sweaty, gyrating bodies, and when he gets there, all this bloke says is "Ow you goin', Adge? All roight?" That's all. Just "Ow you goin', Adge? All roight?" I still laugh at this tale, the way he told it. I liked Adge.'

'The way he told it...' Yes, that's the key to this story, because really, it's not all *that* funny in itself. But by the time Adge had re-enacted the Hurculean battle through the crowd, the gormless question, the Hurculean battle back... Well, it still has Acker Bilk laughing after fifty years, anyway.

Adge's fecklessness as a roadie was legendary. 'Acker's men used to meet in a pub in London, and one of his jobs was to take all their wages in for them,' his manager John Miles recalls. 'He went in the pub, put the bag between his feet and got talking to somebody. Acker said "Come on, Adge, let's get moving," and of course somebody had nicked the bag.' Trombonist John Mortimer, who was with Acker for some twenty-five years and now lives in Germany, laughs when he remembers his leader appointing Adge as 'somebody you can trust' after he had been cheated by a succession of previous road managers: 'Part-way through a tour of Belgium, Adge was enthusing about a bar he'd found selling this strong beer brewed by the monks [*Trappiste*], but his sunny expression changed in a flash when he realised he'd left his briefcase in the bar. Of course, all the band's takings up to that point in the tour were in it. And of course, it was never seen again.'

Another day, after a tiresome journey, the band arrived at their hotel just in time to snatch a few minutes' rest before a show. 'We're the Paramount Jazz Band,' Acker announced at reception. 'I'm sure you are, but you're not booked in here,' the desk clerk replied, at which Adge shrunk to a few inches shorter than his standard five feet seven. But John Mortimer and another old Paramount hand now living in Germany, Rod Mason, agree with their ex-boss when it comes to Adge's entertainment value.

There was he, a non-muso among a set of seen-it-all pros, leading them all in sing-songs on the band bus and reducing them to helpless laughter. Most of the stuff, in which Acker had a hand, was preoccupied with alcoholic over-indulgence: *Dragging My Baby Back Home; I Have Often Crawled Down This Street Before; When The Pavement's So High, It Hits You In The Eye, That's the Scrumpy...*

Sometimes it just got silly. On one of Acker's radio broadcasts Adge was sitting too close to a microphone and the sound of him eating radishes came over the airwaves loud and clear. Word of it went around the BBC and a few days later he was called on to repeat the performance for a children's 'guess the sound' competition. Nobody guessed. Then, on some blasted heath in the ridiculous winter of 1962-63 the band bus got stuck in the snow and Adge hopped out to try to put something under the wheels. Nobody noticed he had gone and the bus got away, leaving him a forlorn little figure in the distance until they caught on. *Stranger on the Moor*, they called him, to his great lack of amusement.

He had very quickly made himself at home in London, a small but – at his best – vital part of a hit-making machine that racked up three more Top Ten entries during his time there: *Buona Sera, That's My Home* and the massive *Stranger on the Shore,* which reached number one and stayed in the charts for fifty-five weeks, making it the best-selling single of 1962. The guys in the band joked about the 'Zummerzet Mafia' being at work when Acker substituted 'And the old zider apples grow' for Louis Armstrong's original 'And the shady pine trees grow' in *That's My Home,* and moaned increasingly that they had thought it was Adge's job to get them out of bed in the morning and out of the pubs for the show, rather than the other way round. Like Acker, they liked his company, but he must have been getting some kind of a reputation; when he was beginning to make it big, one of the music papers had noted that he had 'nominally' been Acker Bilk's road manager. Ouch!

For all that, his younger brother Dave saw first-hand just how much they all loved him in London: 'He went off working for Acker, he thought he was going for a couple of weeks and it turned out to be months, and when he got back his Armstrong Siddeley was still on the side of the road but with all its tyres flat and so on. He asked me and a mate of mine to rescue it, do it up and sell it. We did, and sold it to Bert King, landlord of the Queen's Head in Nailsea. Adge said that as a reward he'd treat the two of us and our girlfriends – I was only going out with Margot at the time – to a great weekend in London.

'We met him in the Horseshoe pub in the West End, and parked the car on the pavement in front of it. Margot and the other girl went off to see a friend, and then we settled down in the pub, after a policeman had come in and said "Who's that with the Somerset registration? You can't park there." We had a couple of pints, then on to the Blue Posts in Soho, where Humphrey Lyttelton played. After that we went somewhere else, met Terry Lightfoot, and so on and on until we ended up at a club where you could stay all night if you had a meal. They would be happy to call a lettuce leaf, a slice of tomato and a finger of toast a meal. Of course, as the night went on, you would get all these people coming back from their gigs. Acker showed up there, Kenny Ball, Johnny Dankworth and Cleo Laine, Bob Wallis and some of his City Gents, most of the England cricket team...

'And there was Adge in the middle of it all, the life and soul. He knew them all – well, perhaps not the England cricket team – and they obviously enjoyed his company. It was a long way from Nailsea, but it was a world he was completely at home in. He lived in West Hampstead, and when we stepped out of his flat he stood on the doorstep to take in the view. "This place is ideal," he said. "Graveyard, pub, betting shop." Not that he used to gamble.'

'British West Hampstead', Adge used to call the place, and sometimes he'd hang a union jack out of the window. The joke wasn't new – in the war the orchestra leader Victor Silvester used to do a BBC forces request show for listeners everywhere 'from British East Africa to British West Hartlepool' – but it tickled Adge, and if a joke tickled Adge he'd always tell it in a way that would tickle everyone else.

Acker and Adge often struck outsiders as more of a comedy double act than boss and employee. They were certainly the best of mates and each of them short and solidly built, they could easily have been taken to be brothers. Another thing they had in common was a profound hopelessness in any kind of practical work, and John

Miles still laughs at a story Adge told him about a visit to Acker's childhood house in Pensford, where his mother still lived.

Acker's mum: Ack, the front door keeps sticking, can you fix it?

Acker: Oh, me an' Adge'll sort that out Ma, no messin'.

(Much cack-handed fiddling around with saws and planes until an inch-wide strip of door lies on the floor.)

One week later

Acker's mum: Ack, there's all this dirt and rain coming in under the door...

Despite all the camaraderie, all the sometimes surreal daftness, Adge was getting restless. He knew his place as a roadie and by now, after all the years of market gardening, minding dad's shop, humping crates of apples and navvying, he at last realised there might be another place for him somewhere else, where he could give full rein to the creative talents the laughter of small audiences had told him he had. Acker's brother Dave had got a few of his songs but had not made any progress in getting them published. 'He just grumbled all the time that nobody was doing anything for him,' says Ted Cowell, a recently rediscovered acquaintance at that time. It was time to take a break, to plan ahead, to sort his head out.

He went to Guernica and lived there for six months, becoming fluent in Spanish. 'I think that West Country burr of his, that drawl, was good for his pronunciation,' Ted suggests. 'He must have been political to go to Guernica. You wouldn't go there otherwise, would you? It's not a tourist destination. It's a very sad place. He was very interested in the Spanish Civil War.' The town's unique place in the annals of bloody conflict in Europe, touched upon in Chapter 2, dates back to April 26, 1937, when Franco called in the German Luftwaffe to bomb it to support his efforts to overthrow the Basque and Spanish Republican governments. Basque figures say 1,654 civilians were killed, German around three hundred. In any event, Guernica was a *cause célèbre*, and while few of those close to Adge suspected him of any deep political convictions, he was idealistic and quixotic enough for the town's embattled history to attract him. To put it more simply, he was always a sucker for the underdog. It is thought that he had already been to Spain at least once before this with his Nailsea pal Adrian Raikes, who had an uncle over there.

'When he came back he was just as unsettled as when he'd gone,' says Ted Cowell. 'At that time I was working with Dave Bilk running a building company called Lyncombe Vale Property and Development in Whiteladies Road. "Why don't you come and work for us for a bit?" I asked him. "Right now we need somebody to drive the van." That suited him down to the ground, so in he came. In fact at that time I was working on a scheme in Spain to get a holiday project going, looking round for a suitable site. Soon Adge was itching to go back there, having made a bit of money on the driving, so I asked if he'd like to do some more work for me, visiting a list of potential sites I wanted looking at. We paid for him to go over with his little Fiat 500 and sent him money as he went along. It wasn't a lot, but it was enough to keep him going. He visited all these places and wrote to me every week, long letters, along with his expenses: "One pencil, one rubber, a postage stamp..." He sent us back the maps highlighting the sites, complete with his comments. We asked him to go to a place called Cartagena and his considered professional opinion was "Shit-hole".

'The Bilks had a building manager, Gordon Sawyer, another Pensford man known as Zank, and he and I left the office one day, bought a Triumph car and drove down to Spain to see him. He was at Calpe on the Costa Blanca, and there was a site down there. I drew up a scheme for it, gave it to Adge to take to the local authorities, and they said they'd never had such a comprehensive plan presented to them, or one so sympathetic to the environment.'

John Miles believes that Adge also played his part in this favourable reception: 'He found this land by the sea between Calpe and Moraira, negotiated with the owner to buy it, and then had to go to the mayors of the two villages to get permission to build. Adge told me he'd visited the mayor of one village one afternoon; they'd sat down and had lots of wine, and when he'd asked whether they'd grant planning permission he'd said "Of course we will. Have another drink." He'd then been to see the other mayor and it was the same story – more drinks, more jolly conversation, no problem about permission.'

Back home it was also looking great: the Bilks were going to put £10,000 into it, so was Ted Cowell, and another £10,000 was coming from a builder's merchant he knew. Then, soon after Harold Wilson's Labour government came in in October 1964, they brought in restrictions on foreign exchange allowances which all but put an end to people going abroad or spending money abroad. 'As far as we were concerned, that was it,' says Ted Cowell. 'Nobody was going to be able to buy a property in Spain again. The trouble was, though Adge's work for us was done – he'd been there six months or so – he decided he was going to be a Spaniard. He started working behind a bar. He definitely wasn't going to come back to England. There was a shack on the beach he was going to buy. It frightened me to death.'

Over years, as his manager, John Miles got to hear all about Adge's little hut on the beach, which he rented for the equivalent of ten shillings a week: 'Every morning, with no money and the bar getting funny because his credit was going up, he would pick up an old tin outside his hut, throw it out to sea and then aim pebbles at it. Over time he got really good, hitting it nine times out of ten – and that's the way he whiled away the day until it was time to go to the bar and persuade them let him have a drink and something to eat one more time. Then, he said, he got up one morning and the tin was gone – "and it was like the end of the world!"' At last he accepted that there was no alternative but to come back to a by now cold, hostile London. He thought his previous exit from Spain had been bad, but now his predicament was desperate – no job, no money and still not the slightest chance of anyone doing anything constructive with his songs. Should he busk on street corners? Would that work? Or might there be possibilities just a rung or two up the musical ladder from that?

Good-time Folk Music

In Wurzels lore it is the accepted wisdom that Adge got back from Spain broke and broken, and it was a visit to his future manager John Miles that changed his life. Only the last part of that is true. John did indeed do everything to create the Wurzels phenomenon, but although not flush with money, Adge was far from broken in spirit when he walked into the Miles Organisation's upstairs offices in Whiteladies Road in June 1966. Since returning to Britain he had taken a good, hard look at himself, shown faith in his songs where others had not and gone around performing them wherever he could. The years of impromptu spots at jazz nights at the Crown and Dove were beginning to bear fruit; untrained as he was, vocally, he had learned how to sing through the buzz of conversation and the fug of cigarette smoke and win over at least some of the crowd with his songs and his sense of fun. It had been invaluable training.

For years Adge's friends had been hearing a constant complaint from him, though it took two different forms. One was along the lines of 'If Chuck Berry can write about Memphis, Tennessee, why can't I write about Easton-in-Gordano, Somerset?' The other was 'I'm tired of going into pubs and hearing people singing *I Belong to Glasgow* and *Maybe it's Because I'm a Londoner*. Why can't Somerset people sing Somerset songs?' He also saw signs that the tide was turning in his favour. His old mate Acker's popularity meant that all the country knew about Zummerzet, and even nearer to home, Coate's cider from Nailsea was on everybody's TV almost nightly, with three lovable cartoon yokels in hats that rather tickled him singing its praises with a tune pinched from Portishead's musical King's Counsel Fred Weatherly.

It is perhaps surprising that when Adge returned to this country in 1965 it was to London; it suggests that at first his thoughts were still on some kind of back-stage role in the music business. It seems that the nearest he got to that was being a night-club doorman (presumably, bearing in mind his height, at a club for dwarfs) but sitting around at home at 82 Solent Road, West Hampstead he quickly realised that only the West Country could give his career the boost it needed. He still had other thoughts vaguely in mind. A chap he met in a club in London thought there might be a future for him in Colombia (the mind boggles), and maybe more out of hope than expectation, he pestered both his jazz-loving friends Keith and Geraldine Box and Bob Ansell, the landlord of the King's Head in Pill, to go to Spain with him, the former because they had a big house in Cotham that they could let for a tidy sum, the latter because he could run a bar that Adge could, er, serve in.

He did, however, have a further, slightly more realistic plan, and fascinating documents pinpointing his progress in the world of music are two very similar letters he wrote to the Swindon Folk Singers' Club and (presumably) another club in the town on February 15 and 16, 1966, offering his services at five pounds per night plus expenses. One says he is 'very well known as a composer and singer of West Country songs' and both flag up forthcoming appearances in 'my own show on BBC West of England radio in March' and 'a folk series on TWW in April'. Each letter goes on: 'Around that time also I am booked into several folk clubs in the Bristol area, and would like to do a few more jobs down that way if possible. I sing all West Country songs, usually unaccompanied, although I could provide accompaniment if required.' Swindon Folk Singers' Club's correspondence is now in the county archives, the Wiltshire and Swindon History Centre, and also includes a letter dated two years earlier from some pushy Yank who was asking for *seven* pounds a night, compared with our Adge's five. Paul Simon or somebody. Flippin' cheek.

Nevertheless, the fact that New York boys were finding it worthwhile to come over here to play – along with the likes of Tom Paxton, Phil Ochs, Ramblin' Jack Elliott, Pete Seeger and Brownie McGhee and Sonny Terry – is a reminder of just how vibrant the folk circuit was in those days. It was also producing homegrown stars who were suddenly making a very decent living, survivors from the Fifties such as Ewan McColl and Peggy Seeger but also a new wave of brilliant musicians, Bert Jansch, Martin Carthy, John Renbourne, Cyril Tawney and the Watersons among them. Redbrick universities and polytechnics springing up everywhere, with heavily subsidised students' unions and hordes of local authority-funded students to fill them, were helping turn folk into, if not mainstream entertainment, then at least a thriving alternative scene. Earn Paul Simon's seven pounds a night plus expenses for three nights a week, and an entertainer was in business.

What Adge quickly realised was that the 'with expenses' proviso, given the material he was performing, would appear far less prohibitive if he was contacting clubs from Bristol rather than London NW6. Besides, a guy he once knew as Ken Colyer's roadie, Howard Rudman, was now working in Bristol as a booking agent and was landing him some decent gigs. He wasn't ready to go back to Nailsea – yet – but returning to the pub and club scene over there would suit him very well, even if the emphasis would be on folk rather than jazz.

An early breakthrough was at the folk duo the Crofters' club at the Bathurst pub in Wapping Road, now the Louisiana. Geraldine Box remembers it well: 'I was more into folk than my husband

Keith was, and my friend Roger White, the resident singer of the Troubadour folk club in Clifton, came to see if I wanted to go with him to hear Fred Wedlock at the Bathurst. Adge was staying with us, and said he would like to come too. In the event, Fred didn't turn up, and the Crofters asked whether anyone from the audience would like to take his place. Adge volunteered, and never looked back from then on.'

The Crofters liked what they heard, and one of them, Gef Lucena, was intrigued enough by Adge to ask him up to his house in Frenchay to find out more. With a tape recorder at hand – he is now best known as the founder of Saydisc records – he had his visitor singing a verse and a chorus of several of his songs into a microphone, and supplying the rest of the words on paper. One result was *Pill, Pill,* named as *Pill Ferry*, appearing – and getting top billing – on the Crofters' first record in 1965, an EP called *Pill Ferry and other Folk Songs*; the other, in the following year, was *Drink Up Thee Cider: The Crofters Sing Adge Cutler*, an EP that also included *Casn't Kill Couch, Champion Dung Spreader* and *When the Common Market comes to Stanton Drew*; all spellings are as they appeared on the record. There was also talk of their recording an Adge song called *The Great Nailsea Cider Bet,* but this did not happen and he must presumably have abandoned it somewhere along the way.

'I thought he had something worthwhile to offer, and the Crofters started performing them,' says Gef. 'I ran the Bristol Poetry and Folk Club, and although we didn't normally have guests, I invited him along. It must have been several months later when he got to us, however, because he surprised me when he said he'd got a group together, and could they come too? I agreed, but when they arrived we were not happy to see they came in amplified, as we were an acoustic club and felt microphones came in between the performer and audience in that quite intimate setting. It wasn't the right setting for the band. It wasn't a successful evening. On the other hand, although he was different, I don't believe the Bristol folk scene looked down on him in any kind of a snobby way. Folk music was pretty earthy, after all, and there would be a good, eclectic mix of Lefties, CND supporters, students and theatre students in the audience. They knew Adge Cutler came along with straw behind his ear and waving a rough stick, but I don't think for a minute that he was dismissed by them as a yokel. He was seen for what he was, somebody dressed for the part of performing earthy country songs. Good songs, some of them, too. I think *When the Common Market comes to Stanton Drew* is my favourite, but I also like *Thee Cassn't Kill Cooch. Drink Up Thy Zider* is closer to the folk tradition, and of course it always goes down very well.'

It must have been evenings like this that Adge had in mind when in later years he told more recent band members hairy tales of the Wurzels' early days on the folk circuit. 'I gathered they didn't like Adge,' says Tommy Banner. 'You'd get civil servants in Arran sweaters singing *I've been a Wild Rover* when the only Rover they knew about was parked in their drive. They'd sing all the traditional stuff, whereas Adge was writing brand new folk songs about the West Country. He was ahead of his time, before regional folk comics such as Billy Connolly, Mike Harding and Jasper Carrott got going.'

Tommy might have added Jake Thackray and Max Boyce to that list, while an almost exact contemporary was Allan Smethurst, the Norfolk Singing Postman who in reality came from near Bury, Lancashire. In truth, all of them, Adge included, had been preceded by the off-beat Scot Ivor Cutler, who Adge never met, so far as we know, but with whom he is occasionally confused today. An early influence on Adge, and one to whom he paid tribute on his *Cutler of the West* album, had been Len 'Uke' Thomas, a grassroots Bristol entertainer who had come up through pubs rather than folk clubs with locally loved 'ballads' such as *Wass Fink Of 'Ee Den?*, *Thee Bissn't Gonna Get'n Out Of I* and *Thee's Better Keep Thee Eye On 'Ee.*

Wass fink of 'ee den?
Wass fink of dis?
Wass fink of 'ee den?
Likewise 'ow bist?

Yes, Adge liked old Len's stuff, and was very happy to give him a little bit of publicity.

What he and all the emerging comedy talents had in common to help them on their way were thriving regional television centres, both BBC and commercial, that had hours of tea-time and late-night slots to fill five days a week and an understanding that talented local entertainers offered a good way to do it. Adge was not kidding the Swindon folk clubs about his forthcoming dates on a TWW folk series in the spring of 1966. *The Cider Apple* went on at 10.30 on Friday nights, and there still exists a clip of him appearing on it, wearing the white jersey with dark (in real life, navy blue) stripes on it that Acker Bilk said made him look like a Spanish troubador. Future Wurzel Henry Davies, who spelled his name Davis in those days, remembers watching the show at home and cringing on Adge's behalf when he was introduced as A J Cutler. Roger White was also on the show, which is now best remembered by those involved for the copious amounts of cider around for the first broadcast. After several rehearsals and re-takes under the studio lights, that was a mistake that was not repeated.

Adge had settled into a one-bedroom top-floor flat at 16,

Pembroke Road, Clifton, when in July 1966 he found himself with a new neighbour in Andy Leggett, who had arrived from London to work as a French-English translator on the Concorde project but would become rather better known in the Bristol clubs as an instrumentalist of great ability. 'There were three more bedsits up there, each with a single bed, a Baby Belling food heater and not much else,' says Andy, who now lives in Germany. 'The other three tenants and I shared a communal bathroom/toilet with a small sash window facing out over Arlington Villas. If you dared to operate the evil-smelling gas geyser over the bath, it spat out fumes laced with hot flakes of corroded copper. In the room directly opposite mine was a shortish, greyish-haired man I thought might be a plumber... A J Cutler. I registered the name on his mail, but it meant nothing to me. The bathroom curtains seemed always to be wet, and I wondered whether he possessed a towel. I played jazz records and sometimes pounded away on a guitar, but we never discussed music until much later.

'On October 7 that year the Troubadour club opened at 4 Waterloo Street, Clifton. I joined the following night and quickly blended into a thriving folk music fraternity, at first as a member of Flanagan's Folk Four, while other singers included Fred and Sue Wedlock and their friends Barry and Wendy Back. I was at the Troubadour on the night when a new band called Adge Cutler's Wurzels was booked to play there, and it was only at some point that night that the penny finally dropped, and I realised this rising star was the A J Cutler I had been nodding to on the stairs. A short while later I persuaded Ray Willmott, the manager of the Troubadour, to book Diz Disley, since I'd seen his folk club act many times in the other Troubadour in London. Adge turned up in the front row of the audience that night with his girlfriend Yvonne, and Disley serenaded her with his ribald and insulting parody of *These Foolish Things*. It was obvious that they were all well acquainted.

'Barry Back, a sound recordist with the BBC West of England film unit, had been roped in to sing and play guitar and kazoo with a jug band being organised by one of his cartoonist workmates, Cliff Brown, a former drummer in Acker Bilk's Chew Valley Jazz Band,' Andy Leggett continues. 'It seems that Adge had explained his idea of a group called the Wurzels to Cliff, and Cliff had gone away with the impression that he was to assemble the personnel. The third member was Quentin Williams, pianist from the Chew Valley band. Cliff was playing jug, percussion and assorted home-made instruments, Quentin, or Q as we called him, sang and played kazoo, more percussion and the legendary ballcockaphone. Adge latched on to Cliff's disappointment when he revealed he'd already put his band together, and as his early career took off he offered to make up for it by giving Cliff, Barry and Q the spot closing the first half of his concerts. A new name was needed, and Cliff came up with the Alligator Jug Thumpers. I saw them at the Wurzels' Colston Hall concert in Bristol in April 1967 and particularly enjoyed their set. A few months later, Q decided he'd had enough travelling; a non-driver himself, he was a very windy passenger. I was invited with my guitar to a party at Cliff and his artist wife Rhoda's home, a good time was had, and I was afterwards informed that the party had really been my audition to replace Q in the Alligator Jug Thumpers, and that I'd passed.'

So Adge's career was taking off – but it made for interesting times back at 16, Pembroke Road: 'I opened my bedroom door one Sunday morning to find Adge spread-eagled, snoring on the landing. Not far away was a plastic container of cider. His suitcase was open beside him, with corduroy trousers, shirt, neckerchief, bits of string and other gear draped over the banister and down the stairs. He woke as I stepped over him heading for the bathroom. "Hello, Andy. Got home late last night. Couldn't find my key," he explained. Being younger and skinnier and a bit dafter than I am now, I lifted the sash of the bathroom window and eased myself out until I was sitting on the stone ledge, about a foot wide, which ran around the building just below the level of the windowsill. With my legs dangling into the void, possibly thirty feet up, I edged my way to the right until I got round to Adge's window, the scariest part being when I had to go round a corner of the building. Luckily, his window was unlocked and I was able to climb in and get his door open. With what I now know about injuries to passers-by caused by masonry falling off buildings in Clifton, I'd never trust a ledge like that again. Yvonne was a frequent visitor, and I was pleased when Adge's success meant he could leave the bedsit, and they moved together into a flat in Tyndall's Park Road. I still have the note he wrote, asking me to return his key to our landlord, Mr Motisi.'

Andy had got to know the Watersons when he was a student at Hull Unversity, and on a return visit after he had moved to Bristol he told Mike Waterson about his new neighbour Adge Cutler. Mike exploded: 'Adge Cutler? I'd like to get him and that Singing Postman and shove one up t 'other for taking the piss out of folk music!'

It was in July 1966 – World Cup month, and the time Adge got his new neighbour Andy Leggett – that he and John Miles started putting together the first Wurzels line-up. That story will be told in the next chapter, but the band's earliest appearances and its first Scrumpy and Western tours belong here, as a reminder that the Wurzels' first ambition was to succeed in the world of folk. One of their first big shows was at the Winter Gardens in Weston-super-Mare, on January 27, 1967 – a sell-out and a rowdy, riotous one at that. Also on the all folk bill, put together by the Troubador's Ray Willmott, were Roger White, Sally (Oldfield, Mike's sister) and Ian, the Crofters, Big Brian from Cornwall and (Ian) Anderson, (Al) Jones and (Eliott) Jackson. The atmosphere was unlike anything Roger had ever encountered, more like a pop concert, and he felt very lonely up there with his guitar as the crowd champed at the bit for the star turns. Gef Lucena of the Crofters also found it unsettling: 'Unfortunately, we sang a couple of their songs, which wasn't very clever of us, when you consider it, and Adge always said we sang them too quickly, anyway. Shortly after that our contacts with him seemed to drift apart...'

An early tour of the Scrumpy and Western show was two weeks in Devon and Cornwall, with Fred Wedlock, Bev and Rich Dewar from Weston-super-Mare, the Alligator Jug Thumpers and Adrienne Webber, who as a teenager was along just for the ride, to find out how these things worked. 'Fred and I knew Adge from *The Cider Apple*,' says Sue Wedlock. 'We had married about three weeks before the tour, and had just come back from a week in the Brecon Beacons when it had poured with rain. One of the things I remember most about it was that the two Wurzels called Reg, Chant and Quantrill, had a row, one hit the other and he was so offended that he refused to go on. They put a red scarf round Bev Dewar's neck, sent him on with his fiddle and he became a Wurzel for a night.

'Adge always had a comfortable bed for the night, but the rest of us had to manage as best we could, on beaches or people's floors. Adrienne was very pretty and only about seventeen, and one of the guys on the tour had taken a fancy to her. When we were sleeping on the beach one night she came and snuggled down between Fred and me for protection! In fact it was Fred who gave her her first break, in a roundabout way. She'd been performing in folk clubs in Bristol, but was not on the bill for this tour. Then, one night, Fred had an asthma attack and she went on and took his spot. He was fine the next night, but they found a slot for her, too, for the rest of the tour. She said she had no decent clothes to wear so all of twenty-four and a married woman to boot, I took her out into whatever town we were in and we looked for a nice dress.'

Adrienne took a leaf from Adge's book, and it was as Aj Webber that she adapted her initials and made a speciality of opening the bill for big name acts on tours and at festivals throughout the world. The Eagles, David Gates of Bread, the Everly Brothers, Crosby, Stills and Nash, Neil Young, Frank Zappa, Kraftwerk, Neil Sedaka (four tours), Frankie Valli and the Four Seasons, Queen and Rod Stewart: all of these and many more can proudly claim to have something in common with Adge Cutler and the Wurzels. Sue Wedlock is still one of Aj Webber's close friends, and never tires of telling the story of how the name change came about. Apparently, when she was using only her first name, clubs booked her because they thought she was a stripper, and were a bit surprised when this little blonde hippy folkie turned up with her battered guitar case. She figured that Adge's name wouldn't give anybody any wrong ideas.

'Adge was a very intelligent man, with a wonderful command of words,' Sue recalls. 'Fred recorded a couple of his songs including *Virtute et Industrial,* which really struck a chord with us, because back then we lived overlooking the Cumberland Basin flyover. I'd been brought up around there, and remember delivering papers to houses that were knocked down to make way for it.'

In the early days, Geraldine Box also viewed Adge primarily as a man of words, a poet: 'I saw him as a Viking warrior waving his sword around, someone to keep out of the way of. He could be so flamboyant and expansive that you honestly couldn't tell whether he'd had a drink or not.' It is hard to believe that when young he was not influenced in both his love of words and his sometimes Rabelaisian ways by Dylan Thomas, one of the great cult literary figures of the Fifties after his scandalous death through drink in New York in 1953. Adge also enjoyed and recited the Dorset dialect works of the rather more chaste Victorian parson poet William Barnes, which reassured him that good regional verse could be taken seriously. Of particular interest is the introduction he wrote for the programme for his second round of Scrumpy and Western tours in the autumn of 1967, with Lyn and Graham McCarthy, the Yetties, Adrienne, Fred Wedlock and the Alligator Jug Thumpers. Its geometric type-setting closely shadows Dylan Thomas's poem *Vision and Prayer*, the difference being that while that work reads as a poem, Adge's simply looks like a piece of prose that's been set funny:

Well folks, it's now a year since the West first resounded to the
music of the Wurzels, and it's spreading already to other parts
of the Country. Of course, we're all very pleased that this
happened, and we'd like to thank all of you who have
made it possible. Also we hope you will continue
to support the 'Scrumpy and Western' sound,
because in this world of pop, it seems
incredible that a regional music and
humour has been placed among
beat groups, ballad singers etc

Adge's longevity as a folk act was considerable – 'good-time folk', he called it – and while it was a little surprising to see an artist of Shirley Collins's standing appearing with the Scrumpy and Western package at Salisbury City Hall in April 1967, we can only be impressed by the Wurzels' appearance at an Easter folk festival at the

Essex Showground in Chelmsford in 1972, sharing the stage with the likes of the Strawbs, Steeleye Span, Al Stewart, Sandy Denny, Gallagher and Lyle and the Watersons. We have sound evidence that that happened. What we have failed miserably to pin down is Adge's much-discussed solo performance at the Cavern club in Liverpool. He must have had some history in the city, since a letter to him from one of his jazzman friends in London dated April 26, 1960 reads: 'On our last visit to Liverpool we missed *Drink Up Thee Cider* and the shower of coppers,' but that is hardly proof that he once trod the hallowed stage, and a Cavern insider insists that the club has rarely, if ever, put on folk sessions: 'Everything but.' Certainly none of the 1,801 bricks in the Cavern Wall of Fame, engraved with the names of 'all the artists' who appeared there from 1957 to 1973, carries any trace of our hero. Despite this, this book's quest for information prompted Dave Jones of Cavern City Tours very kindly to ask around Merseyside's music buffs for an answer, prompting the learned response: '[Adge Cutler was] never a billed singer at the Cavern, and I would guess that the Wurzels have been confused with Wump and his Werbles.' Ah yes, that'll be it. Easy mistake to make.

It's the Zummerzet Zound

John Miles knew of Adge but didn't really know him. To get to his upstairs offices at 81 Whiteladies Road he had to pass by the Lyncombe Vale crew on the ground floor, Dave Bilk and Ted Cowell and all. 'They were all real characters,' he recalls, 'and if you went by in the afternoon it seemed that there would usually be a bottle of wine on the go.' Acker Bilk, a partner in his brother's business, would be around sometimes, and it seemed that a short, tanned, well-built young man would be forever coming and going.

'It was just after Adge had come back from Spain,' says John, 'and one morning in June, 1966 I was coming out of the office and there he was, covered in dust and with a black beret on his head. He asked if he could come and see me, so we went upstairs and he began to tell me the tale of the Spain fiasco and said that since then he had been singing his songs around various places, people seemed to like them but they weren't making him any money. He took a fiver out of his pocket and said "Look, John, this is all I've got to my name. I've got to do something. Can you help me?" Adge and me shook, and that was that.'

In fact it had been back in April that the idea of a band had first come to him, when he dropped into the Midland pub on Midland Road, Bristol, where the landlord was Reg Chant, accordion ace and a well-known face around the Bristol scene. It was a Wednesday night, an evening when two Bristol jazz men, bassist John Macey from the Avon Cities band and guitarist Reg Quantrill, had taken to calling in and jamming with Reg C in the bar, with maybe half a dozen regulars looking on.

'The accordion was hardly a jazz instrument, but we liked the way

Reg could play it in a jazz vein,' John Macey recalls today, 'and when Adge walked in that night I said "Look, Adge, you've got a ready-made backing group here". Soon after that we were getting together and playing a few dates, all for nothing. I only noted professional gigs in my diary, but I remember the four of us rehearsing in a club in Clifton and playing in a pub. We talked about a name and somebody suggested the Mangold Wurzels, but the rest of us didn't like the sound of Mangold or Mangled; so although he might have mentioned it to John Miles, I think we were already settled on the Wurzels.'

John Miles remembers it somewhat differently: 'He got out a piece of paper and he'd written out the name Adge Cutler and the Mangold Wurzels, and told me he'd had this idea that they should wear corduroy trousers tied at the bottom with string, old grandfather shirts, neckerchiefs and waistcoats. So the look, which the Wurzels still have today, was nothing to do with me and all down to him. What I did do was say the name sounded a bit of a mouthful, and he agreed with me that Adge Cutler and the Wurzels would do it.' John booked a gig almost instantly, at the first Pensford Barbecue on June 24, even before Adge had managed to get the gear together. It was also a night on which John Macey was previously engaged with the Avon Cities band, so Adge's old friend Brian Walker stepped in on tuba/bass/sousaphone, as he did on and off for the rest of the year, with or without John Macey in the line-up. 'Squire' Walker later told Yvonne Cutler that he had written in his diary 'the poster printer has given us the name "The Wurzels"'. Though comparative strangers to one another, they came together to put on a show that had the crowd 'spellbound and roaring with laughter'.

Like most people in Bristol Adge knew of a pawnbroker's in Old Market called Raselles, and it was to there that he took his five pounds to go about finding the band's costumes. He certainly got the corduroy trousers there, though how much of the rest of the full rig was bought in the shadow of the three balls is open to some doubt. Since the line-up was already in situ, this goes rather against the much-loved piece of Wurzels lore that Adge bought the trousers first and then looked round for band members to fit them. What we do know is that it was at the Old Mill, Bathampton on July 24, 1966, the weekend before the World Cup final, that the gear was worn for the first time. 'Our first "cabaret", Brian Walker called it.

'Adge chose an appropriate time to come into my office,' John Miles remembers. 'I'd started my business in 1958 at the age of eighteen, and by 1966 I had 350 groups, forty of them in Germany, and employed a dozen people in the office. It was great, but it was non-stop. I felt that in eight years I'd probably slept about eight hours. So I did a deal with Charles H Lockier's company. Charles [a prominent Bristol impresario of the early post-war years] had just died, and his son wanted to keep on the promotion business in Queen's Road. We did a deal in which I passed on all the groups to him, keeping in touch for the first year to tie up any loose ends. My aim then was to find just a few acts and work on them, which I could afford to do without worrying too much about income. The first person to come along, virtually in the next week, was Adge, and I loved the idea. I thought it was fantastic, a great challenge.'

One or two people had been pointing him in John Miles's direction. One was Howard Rudman, the former Ken Colyer roadie who had become a booking agent and had found Adge some of his early solo work. He had worked alongside John and their relationship had ended acrimoniously when the Lockier deal was made, but he knew that Adge needed more management than he or his booking agency could give him, and that John, on the other hand, was looking for just such a project. Adge's old architect boss, Ted Cowell, also pointed him in the right direction – straight up the stairs at 81 Whiteladies Road. 'The two of us would meet up at the Coach and Horses in Highland Square and Adge would tell me of his plans for the band and how best he could go about it,' says Ted. 'He didn't want the Bilks to know anything about it, which put me in a bit of an awkward position. He felt embarrassed about it. Dave Bilk has this Lad Music company, and Adge was disappointed that it had not done more to promote his work. Nevertheless, bearing in mind his long friendship with Acker, he was not sure how they would take his decision to break away.'

So the ball was in John Miles's court – 'and then the realisation dawned. Where was I to go from here? I was just known for pop acts, and this was something different. I was ringing all these places, hundreds of places I used to book acts into, and found myself trying to sell this new act Adge Cutler and the Wurzels to them.'

'What do they do?'

'They sing songs about cider and manure and stuff...'

'You're having me on.'

'Do me a favour, just give it a try.'

John bought a brand new diary for Adge Cutler and the Wurzels, and Adge would go into his office every day: 'He was no trouble, but it's slightly awkward when your acts are sitting there while you're working. Right at the start, when I hadn't got a single booking for them, I was on to the Legion Hall – a place where they used to have punch-ups – at Coleford, the Somerset one, where I'd supplied bands every Saturday night for years and years. I phoned the guy and told him about this new act, and God bless him, he said OK, what about such a date?

'Let me have a look... No, sorry, can't do that one... Fully booked all that week.' 'How about the 1st?' 'No, sorry.' 'The 15th?'

'Well, we've got something then but we can change it. Yes, great, the 15th, you're on.'

'And Adge is sitting there in the corner, looking utterly bemused at first and then laughing and saying "Honestly, you had even me believing we had a full diary." So they got the Coleford gig; a pity all Adge could write about it in the new book he'd bought to record the Wurzels' appearances was 'Wrong venue, entire mistiming of spot'.

'And that was the start of it – but as they got more and more bookings, the problem was that they were not all full-time professionals,' says John Miles. 'Reg Chant, for instance, had the Midland pub on Midland Road, and we'd go there at two o'clock in the afternoon to pick him up and he'd say "I can't come yet, I'm waiting for the brewery. You'll have to hang on." I travelled a lot at first because they were a new act. We got a £25 booking for the Ocean Room in Blackpool Tower [only the Wurzels' fifth gig] and Adge was really excited at the thought of going all that way. He had tripped and broken his ankle so I phoned in advance to tell them that while he could still perform, he would need a high stool to perch on. When we got there, the first thing the manager, a Welsh guy, said to us was: "Oh, 'ello, boyos. You the concert party, is it?"

'Adge looked at me and muttered "Do they know what we do?"

'I assured him they did, and they went down very well, which reassured me that they could be more than just a West Country band. In other areas the audiences looked on them as simply a country, farming act – and even townspeople in the North and Midlands can grasp the idea of that.' Adge's version of events in his date book was 'Not bad considering'.

John Miles's next challenge was to see what he could do about getting the Wurzels a recording contract, and in aiming high and going for EMI he was not entering uncharted territory. Though the Bristol Sound did not catch on nationally, several of his groups had made records and one of them, the Cougars, had had a minor hit with the Swan Lake travesty *Saturday Night at the Duck Pond*. Its producer had been Bob Barratt, who was always up for something different, and when John told him about the Wurzels with his by now well rehearsed cider and manure line, he said 'Well, that sounds good fun, why don't you bring them up to London?'

'He booked studio two at Abbey Road, the Beatles' studio, for a whole day,' John recalls. 'It was at a time when all the record companies had made a lot of money, but they'd also lost a lot of money because three years earlier they'd signed up acts willy-nilly from Liverpool and Manchester, and not all of them had come good. They were a lot more cautious by 1966, so we realised we had to make the most of our big day in London.' What was in the Wurzels' favour was the fact that EMI's Parlophone label had got a lot of publicity, if not massive sales, with *Hev Yew Gotta Loight, Boy*, that Lancastrian singing postman from Norfolk's touching tale of Molly Windley, his little nicotine girl; the label's great inter-office rivals Columbia were ripe for unearthing a novelty act that might go one better.

'We went up in this old Dormobile with its exhaust blowing all the time, and a hole in the floor with a mat on top of it,' says John. 'We'd got props, milk churns and bales of straw and so on, and we packed them all into the van, though Adge wasn't at all sure. "Why do we need them?" he said. "We're just going into a recording studio."

'I told him the plan. When we were on the outskirts of London – no M4 in those days – we'd stop the van and they'd change into the Wurzel gear, and, good as gold, they did it, even though Adge kept muttering that it was all bloody ridiculous. When we drove into Abbey Road they all jumped out, I pushed this milk churn out and it bounced on the tarmac, straw was blowing everywhere in the wind and up in the windows all the secretaries were looking out wondering what on earth was happening.' Doubtless they would have been even more surprised if they had recognised the leader of this weird bunch of yokels as one of the odd but sharp and wise-cracking bunch they'd see in the canteen with Acker Bilk when he was laying down his big hits for Columbia a few years back; wasn't he that funny roadie who used to live three stops up the Jubilee Line from St John's Wood at West Hampstead?

After the kerfuffle died down somewhat and the band members were taking their equipment into the studio, John saw a grey-haired, charismatic looking sort of chap talking to Bob Barratt: 'Bob then brought him over and said to me "I'd like to introduce you to the chairman of EMI, Sir Joseph Lockwood." He said "John, Bob has been telling me about Adge Cutler and the Wurzels, and I've asked him to let me have the tapes at the end of the day." I told the boys the news, and urged them to do a good job. They did, Adge sang all his numbers, and a few days later Bob said the chairman had told him the Wurzels had to be signed. So we got our contract, and Bob said to me that we'd record an LP first, and then take a single off it.

'But where to record it? Adge immediately came up with the upstairs room at the Royal Oak at Nailsea, and the landlord agreed. We worked out we could get about eighty people in, and Bob said we'd put on cider and cheese and get a great atmosphere recording it as live. We sent out invitations, but on the night, November 2, 1966, it seemed to be getting more packed and sweaty, there was condensation running down the walls and Bob began to worry about how many people we had in there. We went over to the door, the person who was supposed to be collecting the invitations wasn't there, so now we had to stop any more coming in.'

Who was that absentee doorman? Step forward Tom White, then a local man in his early twenties. 'The then landlord of the Royal Oak was Don Weston,' he recalls. 'I always used the Oak from when I was eighteen years old, and Don told me I was the man he wanted on the door upstairs for Adge's recording. He advised me that there were so many gold invitations for guests, and to let all of them in, plus a few locals as well. Well, word got around and within a very short time the place was heaving, as I felt I couldn't turn away people I knew. I thought it was a great night, but the next day when I popped in for a pint, Don was cussing and swearing at me for letting so many locals in and barred me from Adge's next recording there. How ungrateful was that?'

Among the journalists invited that night was Mervyn Hancock, then a nineteen-year-old on the *Devon and Somerset News* in Tiverton and later a long-serving news and feature writer on the *Western Daily Press*. This account of the evening is taken from *Wurzel's World*, a book published by that newspaper in 2004. 'For a studio recording you can reckon on allowing thirty minutes or more until the audience warms up and you begin to feel atmosphere,' he wrote. 'For a Somerset pub recording it took thirty seconds. The audience was a cross-section of cider-quaffing Wurzel lovers from every corner of Somerset, from Westonzoyland to Monkton Combe. Nailsea's oldest inhabitant, wearing a top hat for such a special occasion, was flanked by long-haired youths and mini-skirted girls.

'At first the broadcasting men and journalists from rival stations and newspapers eyed each other somewhat coldly; the locals wondered if they should be on their Sunday best behaviour with 'them thar record men from Lunnon in town'. By nine o'clock the press men were clinking glasses like old friends as the TV cameras whirred; by 9.30 the locals were proving that not all the best voices are t'other side of the new Severn Bridge. At ten o'clock we sent out for fresh supplies of cider and beer and the landlord's wife was dancing a Highland fling with Adge; the cameramen complained that the room was too smoky and then lit up fresh cigarettes. At 10.30 the Wurzels did a third encore of *Drink Up Thy Zider* and the Nailsea Mixed Voice Choir raised the rafters on the chorus. Then, sadly, it was all over ...'

Also among the reporters present was the *Sunday Telegraph's* man, who proved how well he had read the press release when the following weekend, under the headline *Brave new zound zoomin up from Zummerzet*, he asked: 'What is sweeping the pigsties of the West Country? What is the pride of Priddy? The boast of Barrow Gurney? What could be "bigger than the Beatles"? It's the Zummerzet Zound... Adge Cutler and the Wurzels (Scrumpy and Western) are being recorded with their Mendip Mazerkas, Shepton Mallet Shanties and Farrington Gurney Fandangoes...

'For EMI took over a Somerset pub last Wednesday to put Adge and his men on wax. "And they even provided the cider," says Adge, wide-eyed. "I reckon people want to hear something out of the mouth of the common man, hear what the common man's got to sing about." And, says Adge, with considerable satisfaction, "They don't come commoner than me." He then launches into the *Chew Magna Cha-Cha*, with old George's milking hat, dung, artificial insemination and all. "He could become the Bob Dylan of England," says the agent who is going to manage Adge's recording career. "If he gets the intellectual nod, he's made!"' Such an enthusiastic and benign welcome from a national newspaper so early in an artist's career can be life-changing, and it was certainly the biggest public boost Adge had had in his career to date, along with a large photograph of him outside the Llandoger Trow in Bristol. Well, you can't expect Fleet Street photographers to stray too far into the West from Temple Meads station, can you?

All twelve of the songs on the resulting debut album, *Adge Cutler and the Wurzels,* were Cutler compositions, refined (if that's quite the word) by him over the years, in some cases a decade or more. It sold eight thousand copies in its first month, which Columbia declared 'an impressive figure for someone known only locally until now'. 'EMI asked what might go on the album cover, and we thought the Wurzels with a carthorse might be a good idea,' says John Miles. 'Adge came up with one called Duke at Isaac Hardwick's Happerton Farm in Easton-in-Gordano. There were pigs on one of the other covers, and they were also at Isaac's. EMI didn't pay him a fortune, but all of sudden he was selling ice creams and cream teas, with Adge Cutler and the Wurzels playing in the background.' The cream teas also got a plug in Bob Barratt's sleeve notes, and he wrote of Duke: 'His favourite singer is Adge Cutler and his favourite food is Wurzels. What an intelligent animal!' (For fuller details of the records discussed in this chapter, see Chapter 12 and Chapter 14.)

But first came a single from the recording, *Drink Up Thy Zider* backed by *Twice Daily,* which reached Number 45 in the *New Musical Express* charts on February 2, 1967 (slightly higher in one or two others) and racked up a total of some 50,000 sales, predominantly in the West Country. The BBC didn't like the risqué B side and banned it, which usually does no harm to sales and can sometimes boost them; John Miles certainly thought this was the case with *Saturday Night at the Duck Pond,* banished by the Beeb for its brutal cruelty to Tchaikovsky but played to death by Radio Luxembourg until it reached the lower reaches of the charts. *Twice Daily* was never going to get major airplay on any station, but John detected a strange phenomenon when the jukebox sales figures came in: 'They'd say something like *Drink Up Thy Zider,* 26,000 plays, *Twice Daily,* 256,000... The jukebox companies told me they had to keep on going round replacing the record not because of the A side but the B side, so they were somebody else who benefited from the BBC ban.'

The recording engineer for the first Royal Oak session was Geoff Emerick, now revered for his work on some of the Beatles' finest albums, *Sergeant Pepper's Lonely Hearts Club Band, Revolver* and *Abbey Road* among them. In his memoirs *Here, There and Everywhere* (Gotham Books, 2006) he noted that *Drink Up Thy Zider* became a number one hit, which makes some people wonder quite how hazy his memories of that night were. Still, it was a mistake in the right direction – and who can find fault in a man who, when asked how he coped and communicated with the Beatles at their most way-out and weird, said it was nothing after working with Adge Cutler and the Wurzels?

For the second LP recorded at the Royal Oak, on May 3, 1967, Bob Barratt said this time it must be definitely invitation only, with no local people let in to swell the throng. Apart from anything else, there was £20,000 worth of equipment in there, and that had been one of the major concerns last time around. John Miles paid two commissionaires to stand at the door and told them clearly that anyone without an invitation should not be allowed in. As the evening went on, however, the room was again crammed for the five-hour session, and the smoky air was stifling. Somebody had cunningly plied the pair with cider, and soon half of Nailsea was in there as before. If that was the case, though, there was still the other half roaming around outside, and shortly after John had taken matters into his own hands and begun turning people away, the repose of the evening was shattered by a brick being hurled through a window. Bob Barratt decided to leave it on the record, between two Adge compositions, *Barcelona Blues* and *The Somerset Space Race,* but in truth it's not too much to get excited about, a tinkle that could have come from a dropped pint-pot followed by a louder jeer. Worse still, the way the record is edited, Adge introduces *Space Race* in a way that makes no reference to the incident. 'It wasn't me who threw that brick in protest against being barred,' protests Tom White. 'But I know who did – and it was somebody else who had been barred by Don Weston!'

In the previous chapter we discussed the early Scrumpy and Western shows that helped launch the Wurzels' career, and before 1966 was out they had also made several live television appearances. The most high-profile was on the *David Frost Programme,* where the only number they were given time for was *Champion Dung Spreader.* 'Fancy being asked to go on a show like that to sing about a load of shit,' Adge marvelled afterwards. On a Southern TV show in Southampton two days before Christmas Reg Chant missed a cue and played an accordion solo right through the weather forecast. And at Granada in Manchester, 'the studio had arranged for truck loads of farm animals to be released as we played,' Brian Walker told Yvonne Cutler some years after Adge's death. 'I milked a little Guernsey cow into the tuba...' For a band just six months old, they were certainly making a name for themselves, those yokels from Zummerzet.

Top left: *The joker of the Clevedon Army Cadets. That's Adge with the kazoo, second from the right on the back row*

Above: *Adge at around the age of eleven, when he moved up to secondary school. Already it's a face full of character*

Left and below: *Adge's old Nailsea haunts as they are today: his father's shop and garage were immediately up the High Street from the Queen's Head, while the Village Institute, where he made his stage debut at the age of seven or eight, is now a Baptist church*

Bottom left: *Adge's sketch of the popular Fifties Royal Princess Alexandra. His art developed into characterful head and shoulders portraits in pastels and on to deft – and daft – cartoons*

Top: In the Army now, on the right of the picture. What did the sergeant-major make of that white shirt peeping out from under his battledress?

Above and left: Two faces of the young Adge – a moody, arty young man and a likely lad from Nailsea out with his mates

Left: It's 1953, and at least they've made it to the cloakroom at the Salthouse in Clevedon. Adge, left, with Colin Blackmore, Wedge Locke, Terry Elverd, his brother Roy Cutler and in front, Roley Hazell

Left: *Man about Barcelona, 1964: Adge crosses Las Ramblas with Fortuna cigarette in mouth, El País newspaper in hand and a hat he must have thought looked the part on head*

Below: *Adge does what a roadie to Acker Bilk's band does best*

Bottom: *Adge often sang at the Royal Oak at Nailsea – most famously in November 1966 and May 1967, when he cut his first two LPs there*

Above: *Adge's float at Nailsea Flower Show, 1956, surrounded by friends and relatives. He is on the far right with trombone and a rather familiar looking hat*

Right: *'I sing all West Country songs...' Adge offers his services to Swindon Folk Club for £5 per night plus expenses in February 1966*

82 Solent Rd
W. Hampstead
London N.W.6
15. 2. 66.

Dear Sir, I don't know if you may have heard of me before but I have composed and sung many West Country songs, I am appearing in April on a folk series on T.W.W and I also have my own programme on BBC West of England radio in March, Around that time also I am booked into several folk clubs in the Bristol Area, and would like to do a few more jobs down that way if possible, I sing all West Country songs, usually unaccompanied although I can provide accompaniment if required. The fee would be £5 plus Ex. So if you have a spare date, please remember,

Yours Truly

Adge Cutler.

P. S. My own songs include :- "Drink up Thy Zider George" "Pill, Pill I love thee Still, "The champion dung spreader" "Hark at'ee Jacko", and many others.

THIS 1937 BEDFORD MOTOR COACH will be driven to London tomorrow (Saturday) by its proud owner, Mr. Roy Cutler (right), proprietor of the Walton Park Garage, Clevedon, and will compete in the annual London to Brighton vintage commercial vehicles run on Sunday.

In London Roy will be met by his brother, well-known Adge Cutler (also seen here) who, accompanied by the group 'The Wurzels' will also travel down to Brighton on the coach.

Roy, who is a member of the Vintage Commercial Vehicles Club, has recently purchased an old fire engine, which he keeps on the back lawn of his home in Halswell Road, Clevedon.

A 'Mercury' picture

Above and left: *The much-loved 1937 Bedford coach. It won a silver cup for being the best-kept vehicle in one London to Brighton rally – then had it taken away again when the judges homed in on all the debris of a Cutler family picnic all over the seats. The coach still does splendid service today at weddings on the Isle of Wight*

Far left: *Adge with his vintage Armstrong Siddeley Sapphire. Another limousine, a Daimler, was so swish that it came complete with glass partition between the front and back seats*

Left: A pre-war Leyland fire engine was another of Adge's treasures. After his death it was bought by a fireman in Yorkshire to be hired out in aid of a firefighters' charity

Below: On tour with Acker Bilk in Germany a bearded Adge took the opportunity to look in on his sister Rita and her husband and two sons, and take them out for a drink with his boss

Above: Adge's last Wurzels: after his death, it was Tommy Banner, Tony Baylis and Pete Budd who took the band to the top of the charts

Left: One of the Wurzels' big breakthrough gigs was the Colston Hall show in Bristol on April 23, 1967. Dave Collett was a close friend from the Acker days, and he hit gold when he co-wrote Stranger on the Shore with his boss. Those appearing at the Queens Hall, Barnstaple on June 14, 1967 included the Weston-super-Mare Dewar brothers and Adrienne, who later had a very successful career as Aj Webber

Above: *Promotions and stunts were all in a day's work. Here the Wassail Queen of Yakima in Washington State tempt our hero with one of her region's apples at the Butcher's Arms in Carhampton in the earl Seventies*

Left: *Party animals: Yvonne Tucker and friends at the Bristol Arts Ball, 1966*

above: How tickled Hi am... Yvonne hams it up with Doddy, Adge looks somewhat bemused

top right: Adge and Yvonne marry in Ringwood, Hampshire in 1972. The only guest is Dick Best, living up to his name as best man

right: Yvonne in the early sixties at the time she grew close to Adge

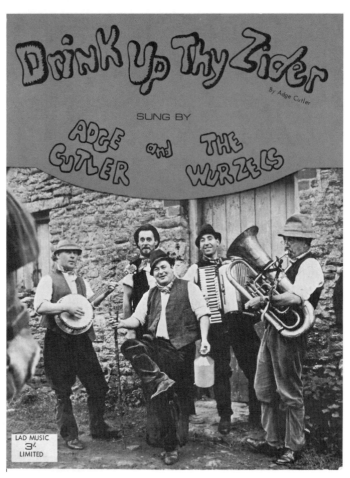

Left: *The sheet music for Drink Up Thy Zider, published by Dave Bilk's Lad Music*

Below: *The presence of the Strawbs at the Wurzel Follies of 1970 at Bristol's Colston Hall pushed the top-priced tickets for this exclusively folk evening up to twelve shillings (sixty pence). At the Winter Gardens in Bournemouth three months later it was very much a variety bill, with Morecambe and Wise and Joe 'Mr Piano' Henderson*

Right: *Drink Up Thy Zider as Henry Davis saw it when he was the Wurzels' musical director*

DRINK UP THY ZIDER

Facing page: Adge plays the part of visiting celeb to perfection at the Bedminster Down Boys' Club's prizegiving evening in 1972 by passing the After-Eights to the lady helpers and signing autographs for the lads. Adge was presented with a splendid cider mug, complete with portrait of Adge with his Wurzel stick

Left: Signs of the times: Adge loved the sound of Nempnett Thrubwell, his favourite of all Somerset's double-barrelled place names, while his eye was also caught by Cowship Lane, near Cromhall in South Gloucestershire

Below: A hard day's night for Adge and the boys at a smoky Ronnie's club in Plymouth. 'Ronnie's – now there was a club,' a veteran fan remembers. 'My head hurts just thinking about it!'

'I'd got fed up with these very serious blokes in folk clubs. So I thought of the name Wurzels, and brought more comedy into it'

When the Wurzels go a'wurzelling . . . homespun songs and rustic ribaldry are never far below the surface. Accompanied by Pete Budd on banjo, Adge Cutler croons about the delights of pig swill. Left: the lads – Pete Budd, Adge Cutler, Tommy Banner and Tony Baylis – entertain club diners . . . a whiff of "Zummerzet" to whet the appetite.

Left: At home at Craigie Knoll, Tickenham Hill, in the winter of 1973-74 with Buster the dog

Above: The TV Times carried a three-page feature on Adge in January 1974, with excellent photographs by Peter Bolton

Right: The demo record discovered by Yvonne's daughter Su. On one side are 1958 recordings of Drink Up Thy Zider and Easton-in-Gordano made at the Royal Oak, Nailsea, on the other In the Haymaking Time, apparently made in Jack Cutler's garage and with Acker Bilk prominent

Left: At home with Yvonne

Below left: Ted Cowell, who found and was allowed to keep the Amazing Vanishing Wurzel Stick

Below right: Buster takes a keen interest in Adge's fine collection of cider mugs

Left: *Keeping the memory alive: Roy Cleeves with his excellent bronzed resin statue of Adge*

Below: *'Somerset Bard': Adge's memorial stone at Christ Church, Nailsea, where his ashes were scattered*

In loving memory of
· ADGE ·
ALAN JOHN CUTLER
1930–1974
"Somerset Bard"
Beloved husband of Yvonne.
"Rest well my love".

The Giant Wurzelrama

From the start it was clear that Adge and the Wurzels would be a big draw at Young Farmers' dances, big barbecues and pig roasts, sports club fundraisers, village shows, country fairs and anywhere where an enterprising local promoter could glance around some farmer's roomy barn and like Mickey Rooney in the old Andy Hardy films whoop: 'Let's do the show right here'.

Sometimes the organisers' idea of what would pass muster was wildly optimistic, and those early days are peppered with horror stories of audiences ankle-deep in overflowing slurry, electrical equipment fizzing and sparking in the rain and other dramas, until John Miles knew something had to be done. 'You could arrive and there was no stage built, and the lighting was a couple of lamp bulbs,' he recalls. 'I said to Adge we ought to do this like a circus, with a self-contained mobile stage unit, and that's what we set about doing.'

A big second-hand furniture van was bought from Bath Autos, and with Adge's brothers Roy and Dave and some others, plans were drawn up to convert it so that its side would flap up to allow for a stage to be pulled out. 'Ah yes, Wurzelrama Productions,' Dave Cutler laughs. 'We did some of it at Black Rock Quarry, where I used to work, and also in the space behind Roy's house. It did good service, that old van.'

'Roy and Dave would turn up in some field in the middle of nowhere, set up and then Adge and the boys would come along when all was good and ready,' says John Miles. 'I remember a night in Martock where we did it in a big field, there was parking in another field and we charged 3s 6d to get in. It was a beautiful night and people just poured in; we had fifteen thousand, and the police

75

were saying no more cars. The deal with the landowner was that we made a donation for the old people of Martock. He left it up to us how much we gave. I think it was £50, and everyone was happy.

'The stage unit made nights like that all the easier, and I felt inspired to aim for even bigger crowds. I wasn't sure Adge alone could do it, so we started going for gimmicky things. One was the World Cider Drinking Championships. It was supposed to be at Sam Sprigg's farm at Weston-in-Gordano, but the field was flooded so we moved it along to Down Road, Portishead instead.'

There was a lot of publicity and controversy surrounding the contest, maybe not to John Miles's utter surprise. A medic told the newspapers that fifteen pints of cider in an hour could kill a man – 'The doctor said stop it, they'll drown!' is how Dave Cutler remembers it – and that struck many readers as perfectly feasible. There was also a high-profile day in court to hear a licensing judge say that as the drinks in the contest were being given away, it was a matter over which he had no control. Needless to say, all the bases were covered when it came to selling the public drinks on site.

The contest was on Saturday, November 5, 1967, Tommy Banner's first appearance with the band. It was still hammering down with rain, and Adge told his manager that if the young Scot stayed with them after this, it would be a miracle. That was the way Tommy was seeing it, too. 'I'd just driven from Scotland, and our only rehearsal was on the Friday at the Bristol Flyer on Gloucester Road,' he says. 'Reg Quantrill was stinking of pigs. His lady friend's father had got a pig farm, and he was going around all the nightclubs in Bristol picking up waste food for swill. You wouldn't be able to do that these days.

'We'd gone through three numbers and then suddenly Reg said right, I've got to go now, and that was it. I was used to busking –

I'd been playing in pubs since I was twelve – but it still seemed a funny way to prepare for a big event with a new band member. The next day things only got worse when we turned up at this field beside the Bristol Channel, freezing cold and lashing with rain. They had us changing in an old wartime bunker which was damp and filthy; judging from what was lying around, it was where half the population of Portishead had been conceived, or narrowly avoided being conceived.

'We did two relatively short spots that night, and of course I just busked the whole show. Adge wasn't a singer, he couldn't breathe properly, so he couldn't last too long on stage. I really was wondering what it was all about. I'd signed this three-month contract – it was hand-written by Adge on a torn-off page from a school jotter with lines on it – and I thought oh well, it won't go on for ever...'

The odd thing, as he contemplated the pigswill and the evil bunker that was serving as his dressing room and the cider-soused contestants rolling about around the stage, was that for this he had turned his back on what amounted to copper-bottomed security and comfort for someone in his business. For seven years or more he had been a fixture on the Lex McLean Show, aiding and abetting Scotland's 'Master of the Belly Laugh', and if two shows a day six days a week over twenty weeks at Glasgow Pavilion, a further twenty in Edinburgh and then further weeks-long stints in Aberdeen and Glasgow did not strike you as a year's good, steady work as a musician, you were in the wrong job.

Tommy Banner was and is clearly in the right job, but nevertheless a young man wants a change sometimes, and during his time with Lex he had occasionally branched out with a double act in the Northern clubs, a date at Accrington Stanley supporters' club being a highspot. 'After that first night with Adge, all I could think was what have I let myself in for?' he reflects. "I'd changed my working clothes from dinner suits to corduroys and wellington boots – and nagging away at the back of my mind was the thought that I had just turned down a contract with P&O to travel the world as a lounge pianist on one of their cruise liners...'

A diary item in the *Bristol Evening Post* a few days before the event had given no inkling of the chaos that would unfold that night. It reported that ten contestants had 'fought their way through heats in the West Country and Midlands', making it seem all so formal and neat and tidy that you expected to read that the proceedings would be compered by Eric Morley in his bow tie. 'Special transport will be laid on to get the contestants home afterwards.'

The winner George Lefeuvre, a twenty-eight-year-old unemployed labourer from Clifton Street, North Weston, was presented with the cup by Adge after he had allegedly drunk sixteen pints of 'the real good stuff' in the allotted hour. George was one of Adge's old power station workmate 'Weasel' Holder's young drinking cronies at the Anchor in Portishead, a fact for which the older man tried to take credit, but which in truth embarrassed him greatly. A regular eighteen or nineteen-pint-a-day man, so say, Weasel disgraced himself and dumbfounded his backers by sinking just four pints in the hour, and young George doing four times better than that was hard to bear.

Allegedly four times better. George Rollings, in his recorded conversations with Mel Gordon, would have none of it: 'They 'ad a cider drinkin' contest, but I was on the cider so much I couldn't do it,' he grumbled. 'George Lefeuvre won it, but most of it went on the floor, all over their trousers. They said 'ee drank seven or eight pints of the real good stuff. A lot said 'ee didn't, you know how 'tis. Weasel entered the competition, and his face ended up looking like bloodshot sandpaper. I never seen nothing like it. It was all over the front page of the *Mirror*. Anyway, George got off the stage, fell down on top of the cup and flattened it. So 'ee chucked it in the water. It's still out there, far as I know.'

In fact it's not still out there at all. The *Western Daily Press* photographed him with it, along with Weasel and a couple of their mates, a few days later. Mind you, it does look a bit battered and bruised; perhaps Weasel did his famous trick of diving in to rescue it, fishing out an extra penny or two along the way.

Two urban myths survive the cider drinking championships. One is that Adge wrote *Drink Up Thy Zider, George*, to commemorate this evening, though as we have seen, the song had been written some ten years earlier or maybe more in honour of George Rollings, who was so drunk on cider on the day of the championships that he could not take part; in his eyes, that would probably have added up to some kind of moral victory. The other story that still goes the rounds is that alongside the report of George Lefeuvre winning the cup, the newspapers carried another about the police arresting him for being drunk and disorderly. We are unable to verify this, but a tale that certainly rings true is that immediately after the contest the Anchor crew headed back to the pub to continue the night in their accustomed manner. Weasel, after all, had some catching up to do, and some egg to wash off his face with scrumpy.

The World Faggot Eating Championships followed in 1968, a tie-in with Mr Brains Faggots, for whom Adge had recently sung *Faggots Is The Stuff* for a TV commercial. 'We couldn't move for faggots for weeks on end,' his stepdaughter Su Elliott says. Again there were 'regional heats' at one of which, at Hereford Racecourse, a giant of a man called David Jones from Vowchurch scoffed twelve of them in five minutes. That was all fine and dandy, and a good time was had by all, but it was back to full-voltage publicity for the World Muck Spreading Championships at Sprigg's field on September 6, 1969.

By this time the Wurzels were in full stride, and there were warnings on the poster to come early, as the ground had a 'Limit of 90,000'. Not only the band but their manager were having the time of their lives, and today John Miles looks back on these years with pure delight. 'I loved the whole buccaneering spirit of it all,' he laughs. Whatever trick he pulled, it worked, as the former *Western Daily Press* reporter Maurice Fells admits: 'How can we forget those world championships – cider drinking, dung spreading and so on – and the big crowds they pulled in? We all fell for it. John was like Max Clifford in those days.'

The declared aim of the championships was 'To Find The Champion Muck Flinger (Spectators Watch At Their Own Risk)', and on a poster for the evening 'The Giant Wurzelrama' stage now got a billing of its own. Altogether, with a bar, hot dogs, chips and skittle alley on the menu, it didn't seem to add up to a bad night's entertainment for 7s 6d, even before you accounted for Adge and the Wurzels and their support act the Roman Remains.

One man who did not need a second bidding to come early was Hector Hamer, another of Adge's old mates on the Portishead B site, whose life changed forever when he came third at flinging the dung. Or maybe not; he remembers his reward being a couple of pounds. 'I saw this big poster pinned up on a telegraph pole and was so intrigued to see what it was all about that I turned up in the afternoon,' he says. 'I found some rugby posts had been put up in front of a great heap of dung, with a light bulb hanging off the top of one of them. No sign of Adge's Giant Wurzelrama, but when it grew dark, there he was, singing away. Then, towards the end, when everybody had had a few, he launched these great muckspreading championships, so up I went to see how I got on.

'The idea was to get some muck on a shovel, stand behind a line and see how far you could get it over and beyond the crossbar. One or two had a go with a floppy load of manure that didn't even reach the bar, but some of us latched on to the fact that if you got a handful and made yourself a cannonball, it was good to go for miles. The trouble was, there were crowds of people lined up to watch, and there'd be shouts of dismay from one side or another as somebody's shot flew wide.' Hector admits that he has rashly spent his two pounds prize in the forty-odd years since then – but he kept the poster, which is now framed for posterity.

Not all John Miles's ventures bore fruit. 'With outside barbecues we were always getting maybe a thousand people climbing over the fence,' he recalls. 'We tried playing at racecourses, where there were turnstiles and security people, and we went to Wincanton, Hereford and Chepstow. They were OK, but the atmosphere wasn't quite right, and Adge said he didn't want to do them any more.' John's downstairs neighbour in his offices in Whiteladies Road, Ted Cowell, also came unstuck when he felt he could make money with a big outdoor event near Ross-on-Wye, starring Humphrey Lyttelton, Adge's Wurzels and a pop group, 'It was all on that portable stage of John Miles's,' he recalls. 'We also had a huge marquee in case it rained, portable dressing rooms and showers. Absolute fiasco, it was. Something like three thousand people turned up, and I was expecting thirty thousand. I'd managed to arrange it for when there were all kinds of big festivals all over the place. Worse still, I had a manager called Rod Dowells. He came to see me and said "When I tell you what I've got to tell you, you can sack me on the spot if you want. I've done something awful. I gave the wrong people the money for the pop band. It was on the table, all ready, and a guy came in in these motorcycle leathers with his bike outside, and I thought he was their roadie. I told him all the money was there, he tucked it in his pocket, said thanks very much, got on his bike and was away. Then the real roadie came in..." It's odd how things take you. I wanted to burst out laughing, rather than crying, because we'd lost a fortune, anyway.'

More profitable by far was the spectacular spin-off from the Giant Wurzelrama that became the transport for the *Radio 1 Roadshow*, with John's brother Tony increasingly involved both backstage and on air, where Smiley Miley's name was for years as familiar to listeners as any of the DJs'. The first *Roadshow* vehicle, which made its debut in Newquay in July 1973, is described on radio nostalgia websites as 'a caravan built and hired by brothers John and Tony Miles'. By the time the show reached the end of the road in 1999 Tony had risen to the post of tour manager and two giant trucks reversed back-to-back formed an impressive seventy-five-foot frontage and space enough for a 'green room' for interviews and get-togethers. It was all a long way away from Black Rock Quarry.

But one question remains. Forty-five years on, what has happened to Tommy Banner's early misgivings? 'By the time my three-month contract was up, I could see there could be a good future in what we were doing,' he says. 'What's more, Wurzels music is enjoyable to play, and that's so important.' Equally so is the fact that they don't have him changing in storm-blasted concrete bunkers these days.

The Amazing Vanishing Wurzel Stick

Thanks to John Miles, the Wurzels were never out of the news. It seemed that before every big gig or if Adge's smiling face had not appeared in the press for a couple of weeks, some terrible wrong would befall them – but nevertheless, despite it all, they would soldier on and be at the Spa Hotel on Saturday night, seats still available from 4s 6d to 8s 6d, full supporting cast, come early to avoid disappointment.

Would you believe it, the show even went on after Adge had lost his *Wurzel stick*. How's that for fortitude? 'After that, I insured it "against all risks except woodworm" for £100 through General Accident,' John laughs, reliving his enjoyment of this stunt and dozens more. 'Oh, he was always on to the *Post* or *Press* with some tale or other,' the veteran Bristol reporter Maurice Fells groans. 'One day we were sitting in the *Press* newsroom when the phone rang and John was on telling us of his deep anxiety that the Lord's Day Observance Society had somehow got wind of the Adge Cutler show at the Colston Hall on Sunday (seats still available) and were going to protest. Well, whoever could have tipped them off about that, we sniggered to one another. But we used it, and it caused a bit of a fuss, and of course John had the Colston Hall packed to the rafters come Sunday night. As for Adge losing his Wurzel stick, you'd have thought the Crown Jewels had gone missing. He even got it on *Police Five*, between reports of the thefts of jewellery and a lorry.'

In fact it wasn't stolen at all, but merely mislaid. 'It was on the Isle of Wight where he left the Wurzel stick behind,' Adge's architect chum Ted Cowell remembers. 'I'd built a dolphinarium at Sandown, and my wife Molly and I went to see him playing at Ryde. A couple of days later I got a phone call from him. '"Ere Eddard," he said. "I've left that bloody Wurzel stick be'ind." I said I'd go and collect it right away, which I did. I thought he'd be really happy, but all he said when I told him was "Oh, don't you worry, Eddard, I've had another one given me." It rankled a bit, but that's why today I'm the proud possessor of one of Adge Cutler's Wurzel sticks.' It was Rowley Ansell, a gamekeeper near Failand and one of Adge's pub buddies in Pill, who was Wurzel-stick-procurer-in-chief, searching around the copses for suitable lengths of blackthorn with bifurcated ends. Ah, 'bifurcated', there's a word Adge would have enjoyed. Life in the Wurzels would doubtless have gone on without one, but most people's memory of Adge on stage takes in that Wurzel stick leading the choruses and laying down an approximation of the beat. Occasionally he put it to good use repelling boarders. One night the mic went silent, a hapless technician crawled to Adge's feet proffering a hand-held one, and all he got for his troubles was a beating about the head with a Wurzel stick.

There was mileage, too, in Coate's cider works in Nailsea naming one of their big vats after him. For years they had been honouring famous personalities in this way, and a three-page colour feature in TV Times in January 1974 was headlined *What put Adge's name up there with Churchill and Stalin*? What helped put it up there, in truth, was the fact that the publicity-minded Coate's liked the idea that John Miles had persuaded the Pathé Pictorial cinema feature people to film the naming ceremony, along with an impromptu concert held in front of the vat by all five early Wurzels. 'We all met at Coate's early one morning for the unveiling, and there were bales of straw to sit on,' John recalls. 'There was also cider, and plenty of it, which is why the film, taken at the end of endless rehearsals and takes, is notable mainly for the untidy group of largely inanimate, red-faced men slouched around the place.' Not only the audience was affected, and though Adge and the boys look lively enough, the sounds they were making made it necessary for their songs to be dubbed on later.

As we have discovered, Adge and the Wurzels moved very quickly on from country gigs in the West to the cabaret circuit, regularly taking in parts of Britain for which they cared nothing. It was a hard slog, but the kind of money being paid by the jewel in the circuit's crown, the Batley Variety Club in Yorkshire, was a reminder that these were no mere working men's clubs. The likes of Jayne Mansfield, Louis Armstrong, Roy Orbison and Tom Jones could look forward to a pay packet of £4,000 a week to play Jimmy Corrigan's club built on top of a sewage works, and while Adge was never remotely in that league, he knew that part of the world could not be ignored. 'He had to change the style of his show,' says the booking agent Howard Rudman. 'He struggled in clubs at first, but he got there in the end.' He was a quick learner, too. 'He got friendly with Ken Dodd, who told him "Forget about a laugh a minute. It's got to be a laugh every ten seconds," and he took that to heart,' says the former Wurzel Henry Davies. Still in a suitcase at Adge's stepdaughter Su Elliott's home are notebooks crammed with random ideas, spoof song titles, silly insults, anything to get a laugh. One of them is an address book, with scores of entries for every letter of the alphabet: *Abominable Yeoman, Damsel in Dis Dress, Engelbert Scrumpy-Stink, E-Type Dung Cart, Gone with the Wind by Michael Rennie, I was Yul Brynner's Head Polisher, Last of the Long Trifles, Silage is Golden, Strawberry Fields for Cheddar, The Thoughts of Airman Chow, Take the Hay Train, Ultimate Detergent...* Nobody could accuse Adge of not taking being funny seriously.

'When he first started, it wasn't all success by any means,' his brother Dave recalls. 'He was doing a show at Lynton, I went down with him to be on the door, and they had about six people there. On the other side of the coin, I remember there was a gig at the Spa in Clifton that was absolutely heaving. You couldn't move.' An even bigger gig in the early days was the half-time entertainment at Bristol City's fourth round FA Cup tie against Southampton at Ashton Gate on February 18, 1967, where the Wurzels got the second-biggest cheer of the day from the 38,017 crowd, eclipsed only by the racket that greeted Terry Bush's winning goal. In later years the Wurzels and City became interlinked, not least because of Tommy Banner's passion for the game, and *Drink Up Thy Zider* and a rewritten *Morning Glory* became anthems on what used to be called the terraces. Adge, however, took only a passing interest in both football and City. *Virtute et Industrial*'s line 'If City don't win Saturday, perhaps the Rovers will', tells us all we need to know.

As time passed and his confidence grew, he came to feel more at home north of Tewkesbury. 'On stage in somewhere like Birmingham he knew some woman or other would always laugh out loud when he announced *Pill, Pill*,' says John Miles. 'He'd say "No ma'am, it ain't what you're thinkin'," and go on to paint a picture of this beautiful little Somerset village with its boats nestling down by the river...' Some gags, on the other hand, defied translation.

'Someone said to me that was your last LP. This next one must be your *Lord 'Elp 'Ee.*'

Silence.

'Zummerzet joke, that.'

Even when he reached the heights he did, Pill remained a special place for Adge – no sleepy fishing village, but a community bound up with the sea, in tradition at least, in a way few others are. The home of river and dock pilots and their helpmates, the hobblers, it was once fiercely working-class and boozy, happily supporting twenty-one pubs and cider houses. 'I rode over to Pill, a place famous from generation to generation... for stupid, brutal, abandoned wickedness,' the founder of the Methodist Church, John Wesley, noted in October 1755, but when Adge rode over there, right to the end, it was with a light heart. 'He used to spend a lot of time in Pill, usually at the King's Head,' says Dave Cutler. 'You hear a lot of people saying he was always in the Star, but it was more often the King's Head.' For Howard Rudman, another pub is the one he most associates with Adge: 'I lived at Sea Mills and used to go over on the ferry to Pill on Sundays to watch them rehearsing at the Duke of Cornwall. There was some drinking done at those sessions, and Adge always seemed so relaxed and happy there, completely at home. I still think *Pill, Pill* is his greatest song.'

It was comforting for Adge to be back among these people, since he found some aspects of his new life hard to handle – the travel, the absurd hours, the 'biz' side of showbiz. 'He *was* a businessman,' says Henry Davies. 'He was a good businessman, and he had ambitions.' Nevertheless, there were times when Adge looked back on the times when writing verses on the back of Woodbine packets was fun and easy. Now, even after he had graduated to notebooks, it wasn't really either any more. He still wrote, constantly, but it was more quick one-liners to keep the audience's attention, rather than raw, rustic ballads and songs of love to a rural Somerset which throughout his lifetime had been more myth than reality, anyway. He blamed the pressures of his lifestyle for hampering his ability to write new material, yet that particular creative power had begun to slip away from him years before. The twelve songs on the first LP were all his. There were still half a dozen on the second, but after that his presence as a songwriter diminished quite rapidly. He grumbled to Henry Davies and others about the record producer Bob Barratt padding out the albums with music hall and rugby numbers – *Sweet Violets, Oh! Sir Jasper, The Wild West Show, The Marrow Song* – but if he had been turning out material up to his old standard, Bob would have been welcoming it with open arms. 'We had fun putting *Cutler of the West* together,' Henry recalls. 'I thought it would be nice to have examples of all twelve major keys on the record, maybe just with odd chords in verses, and I wanted to experiment a bit with the single *Don't Tell I, Tell 'Ee* that was out at around that time, asking Reg Quantrill to play in B. "I can't play in B." "Yes you can, do B flat and go one fret up." And it turned out fine.' Henry also has happy memories of *I'm the Captain of a Dredger*, which was planned as the Wurzels' first single post Adge, was never released and instead was put on the *The Wurzels are Scrumptious!* LP. 'I wanted to give it a Gilbert and Sullivan, *Pirates of Penzance* feel,' he remembers. That is what he did, and the record also made a funny video.

'In his early days, Adge had an innate ability to get a good melody, one that might have drawn on a variety of sources but was nevertheless his own,' says Henry Davies. 'But in the end he was running out of tunes, so I worked on them with him and we shared the royalties. There were others I worked on where I wish I *had* shared the royalties!'

Despite these creative problems, Adge's new life had compensations beyond the big house on the hill and a ready escape route to Spain whenever he had a few days off. He had always had an eye for cars, not necessarily fast ones, and to these he added various other vehicles. His elder brother Roy remembers that his first car was a 1934 two-seater Singer, but others came thick and fast in the twenty or so years before the end: a Bedford Dormobile, a little Fiat in which he buzzed all over Spain, an alarming sounding Hudson Terraplane, a Humber Super Snipe, a 1934 Daimler limousine, a 1936 Packard, a 1933 Invictor, a 1929 Manchester bus, a 1935 Albion lorry, a metallic blue Alfa-Romeo, and the Bournemouth-registered MGB with its pleasing XEL number plate in which he died. He'd have said the Alfa was the jinx car. It was broken into once, run into when parked, once in Spain, and fallen on to by a tree after it had refused to start. Adge thought a change of colour might do it good, so had it sprayed cream, and on its way back from being made over at Roy Cutler's garage somebody ran into the back of it. That broke even Adge's resolve. 'Bad luck, that car,' he moaned. 'I'm gettin' rid of 'ee.' Andy Leggett, Adge's former neighbour in Pembroke Road and a professional translator, remembers helping him with correspondence 'when he was spending the Wurzel proceeds on those vintage cars he was importing from the South of France.'

Always sentimental when it came to old Nailsea, he would have loved to have been able to buy back one of his father's Bedford coaches after the business was sold to West of England Motor Services, but it was not to be. Instead, in 1967, he bought a near-identical model, a twenty-five-seater 1937 Bedford WTB with coachwork by Duple, registration JT 8077. It is now one of three vintage coaches run by John Woodhams Vintage Tours of Ryde, Isle of Wight, and John says it is particularly popular when it comes to carrying wedding guests from church to the reception. 'We used to tell people it was Adge's band bus, but we know now that that isn't true,' he says. 'What we do tell them is that it's in such good condition because it's been pickled in cider.' Adge bought it from its original owners, South Dorset Coaches of Corfe Castle, but it became semi-derelict after Roy Cutler sold it after Adge's death. Back in Dorset, it was expertly restored by Pearce, Darch and Willcox of Cattistock, and sold to John Woodhams some twenty years ago. The Cutler brothers occasionally took it on rallies, including the London-to-Brighton commercial vehicle run, but Adge's stepson Bob Tucker has far clearer memories of both families being packed in for trips to Weston or Burnham.

Adge also bought a fire engine. As you do. It was a 1939 Leyland Tiger that had been based at Redditch, one of those splendid old things with great wheels for the ladders on the back, a design obsolete by the late Fifties. After he died it found its way to Wakefield, where a fireman restored it and took to hiring it out for weddings and parades to raise money for firefighters' benevolent fund and Yorkshire air ambulance. What made all this easier, for a man who hardly knew one end of a screwdriver from another, was the simple expedient of going into partnership with his motor mechanic brother Roy, whose garage in Clevedon could keep everything up to scratch and also provide ample storage space. When the menagerie grew too big, some of the vehicles went to Russ Conway's brother's garage, which was also in Clevedon, and there was great relief when a big fire there left them unscathed. Pub quiz question: In which town did Russ Conway and Adge Cutler's brothers each own a garage?

As the money started rolling in, there were also the good times, the entertaining, the parties, especially after he and Yvonne had moved into a good-sized flat in Tyndall's Park Road, Clifton. The number of people in Bristol who still remember one in particular is remarkable, and it really must have been quite a night. This is Dave Cutler's version of events:

'Adge had been to Spain, and it was his birthday. The breathalyser had just come in. The Wurzels were playing at the Spa in Clifton, and afterwards Adge invited us back to the flat for a party. It was a big night, and another act performing locally that evening was Allan Smethurst, the singing postman, who also found his way there. Adge had got barrels of wine and cider all along one wall, and a good time was had by all.

'My wife Margot had drunk quite a lot and I decided we should go home. It was early in the morning and everywhere was thick with frost. I knew I couldn't risk driving, but Adge's friend Dick Best offered to take us down to the station, at which Allan Smethurst put Margot over his shoulder like a mailbag and we somehow managed to get her in the car. Down at Temple Meads we had quite a wait for the Weston train, and Margot was still well out of it. "Blimey, you're going to have trouble with her," a porter said, and he was right. There wasn't a taxi to be seen at Weston, and as we made our long way home on foot, Margot cursed me every step of the way. Despite that, though, this is a wonderful memory of Adge's time in my life. Looking back, the whole of that night was just perfect – the gig, the party, everything.'

Henry Davies remembers it best for his meeting with the Norfolk singing postman. 'He was performing at Hickey's club in town,' he says. 'He had a guitar style borrowed from Woody Guthrie, but he wasn't a particularly good musician and unlike Adge, who had been around the business for years, he really was somebody who'd come out of a sheltered country background. He didn't seem to be coping very well, and years later I wasn't surprised to hear his life ended as it did.' Allan Smethurst had a drink problem, and spent his last years in a Salvation Army hostel in Grimsby before dying from a heart attack in 2000.

The Wurzels gimmicks continued, and the Local Government Act of 1972, which redrew many county boundaries in England and Wales from April 1, 1974, was also fertile ground, with Somerset's northern reaches divided between three new districts: Woodspring, where Nailsea was, Wansdyke and Bath. 'The Woodspring MP Sir Paul Dean had called a public meeting in Weston-super-Mare, and Adge was up on stage as part of the panel,' John Miles remembers. 'Maurice Fells of the *Western Daily Press* was there, and I told him I planned to give him a good headline by shouting "Adge Cutler for President of Somerset!" It was getting quite late and Maurice said look, I'm up against my deadline here. So I shouted it, and everybody laughed and cheered, and so the Save Our Somerset campaign was born. Of course, how ten tons of cow dung got to be dumped outside Sir Paul's gate shortly afterwards, nobody could possibly imagine.' That's the story as Maurice Fells remembers it, too – with one exception. 'Was it John who shouted that?' he asks in some surprise. 'I thought he'd been told about it in advance, and somebody else was doing the shouting. I'm not sure I'd have gone along with it if I'd known it was *him*! But it was certainly a funny meeting. All these anti-Avon protesters and po-faced councillors. There was uproar in the audience when the shout went up – but not among the bigwigs on the stage.'

Adge seemed a bit embarrassed by it all when he was interviewed at home for the local TV news next day. 'We're not after independence or anything like that,' he explained. '[President of Somerset] is just an honorary title.' By this time he was presenting a tweedy, country squire image to the world when he was in civvies, and was increasingly sedate looking for a man in his early forties. He was certainly happy to play the part of local celeb, and supported many good causes in one way or another. For instance, he twice visited Bedminster Down Boys' Club, in 1967 and 1972, presented the prizes and was full of praise for a production the lads put on. 'You might have a hit there, Steve,' he told the producer.

His relations with the press were also largely cordial, apart from the odd blip. 'I remember interviewing him in the late Sixties in the canteen of the old *Post-Press* building in Silver Street,' says Maurice Fells. 'For some reason there was no question of taking him out for pictures, so the photo showed him with a cup of canteen tea. It was a decent enough interview, but I remember all the way through it I was thinking who is this man? What does he really want? Is it *really* fame he's after? He seemed a decent chap, but my over-riding feeling was that I found it hard to figure him out.'

Tim Davey, then (and still) of the *Evening Post*, says: "I don't know what sort of a bloke he really was, but I remember being mightily impressed by his public persona back in the early Seventies when I first arrived at the paper. I was sent to Stanton Drew to do a piece about the impact our joining the Common Market would have, and being daring and innovative in that callow, youthful way, I rang John Miles to ask for the lyrics of the song to slot between my pungent paragraphs. He didn't know and told me to ring Adge. I got the impression no one had ever really written them down, but he was charming and just reeled them off (v-e-r-y s-l-o-w-l-y) for me.'

Towards the end of his life Adge Cutler was a household name in much of Britain, and had begun to make some inroads overseas. His last single, a cover of the Fifties American rock number *Little Darlin'*, was released in France, Germany, Holland and even Japan, and then there were the talks aborted by his death about TV with Granada in this country, dates in Germany and a tour of Canada. Just what might have come of these it is impossible to tell. In many ways Adge's career had not progressed significantly for years. His records, both singles and albums, were becoming fewer and farther-between; his tour of Germany early in 1974, immediately after the arrival of Pete Budd, was to forces bases, and you don't have to be an international superstar to play those; and after all, on that fateful Sunday morning he was returning from the Crystal Room in Hereford, not the London Palladium.

And yet, and yet... His act was still in big demand – there was scarcely a day off throughout 1974, apart from his month in Spain planned for October – and there genuinely had been a big breakthrough on national TV in the months before he died, with a repeat series planned. 'Adge had done a few things on HTV with people sat around on bales of straw, that kind of thing,' John Miles remembers. 'Then this producer said he'd got a lunchtime slot on national TV. Adge did the series, and the response was tremendous. He was now nationally known, and it was all beginning to take off. His fan base was obviously still mainly in the South West, but now the word was spreading, and I knew national fame would come. I know that if he'd lived he would have been completely loved nationally. He would have been enormous. He would have been an icon. He was talented in many ways, though he knew he wasn't a brilliant singer. I feel he'd have been like a Johnny Cash figure.

'Once he had two gigs at the Council House in Bristol on successive nights, the Dustmen's Ball followed by the Lord Mayor's Ball. He was exactly the same man at each event, and each crowd loved him just the same and sang along with his songs just the same. That gave me another reason why I was convinced that he would have been enormous.'

The producer John Miles refers to is Charles Wallace, an Australian still at work and living in London. 'I went to HTV as a freelance in the summer of 1973 and agreed with the boss there, Patrick Dromgoole, to do a pilot music and entertainment for a lunchtime network spot,' he recalls. 'Looking around for local talent, Adge Cutler and the Wurzels were a very obvious choice – at least, to me – and it soon became clear that Adge was a good front man for the show. It's important to have somebody to do that, to be able to say hello to an audience and make them feel welcome. It's an underrated ability, but it's one Adge had. They were not a unanimous choice. I'd done television pop shows in London and felt well up for this one, but a lot of old hands in the West said "Oh, steer clear of the Wurzels, they're on everything, they've been done to death." As soon as I saw them, though, I knew they were what I was looking for.

'We also had a two girls and a guy Seekers, Peter Paul and Mary type of trio, called White on Black [Sue Franklin, Jon Knowler and Suzi Lawrence from Hartcliffe, Bristol], along with Fred Wedlock and the Pigsty Hill Light Orchestra. We called the pilot *Up the Clump*, after Adge's song, but the network thought that had unfortunate connotations and changed the name to the *Great Western Musical Thunderbox*, which we thought was hardly any better. We did half a dozen shows, mainly in a studio decked up like a barn but with a couple of sequences filmed on location. We had Pigsty Hill in the Pump Rooms at Bath and the Wurzels on Glastonbury Tor and – unforgettably – in grass skirts out by the muddy Severn Estuary for *Aloha, Severn Beach*. Adge didn't fancy that at all, worrying that this wasn't his image, but he went along with it. It was an eventful time. We had Leo Sayer in the studio right at the beginning of his career, and some nuns complained to the IBA after Fred had sung a song called *Sister Josephine*, about a police raid on a convent.

'I resigned five times and Patrick Dromgoole fired me once, but the show was going down well all over the country and when the network commissioned another thirteen, I was more than up for doing them. Then Adge died, and everything changed. It was decided the series should go ahead, but shortly afterwards I left HTV for Central, and in the end I think there were just a few more shows. His death killed the series. Their manager wanted us to use the boys without Adge to front the series. That, of course, is what happened with their live shows, and it worked out well for them in the end. But this was television, and it was all so close to his death, and I said I wasn't sure it was right. I thought that then, and I do now.' In the event, Fred Wedlock took over, and in time he became a very able and amiable presenter of a variety of shows for HTV. But Adge's passing had dealt the *Thunderbox* a fatal blow, and it was time for Charles to move on.

Would Adge have gone on to greater things had he lived? Charles Wallace is certain he would. 'I don't know about Top Ten hits, but I'm sure he could have become a big TV star, a top novelty act,' he says. 'Those shows were going down so well on the network with Adge fronting them, I know he could have built on that. Adge Cutler and the Wurzels were an act waiting to be discovered by the wider world. Those few *Thunderbox* shows half discovered them. If it had gone to another thirteen, who knows? Adge was certainly willing to learn. He was used to being in charge, he had his own way of doing things and if you presented him with something a bit different, he would not be so sure. But as with the grass skirts at Severn Beach, he was willing to accept that television was a new medium to him, and to put himself into the hands of the professionals. He was already good, and he could only have got better.'

The Boys in the Band

L ife full-time on the road was a culture shock for the prototype
Wurzels, all of whom were musicians of professional or at least
semi-pro standard who had honed their craft in the Crown and Dove
and other Bristol venues. They had known Adge as a performer far
less polished and experienced than themselves – the cheery guy who
stood up and did a number or two while they were having a fag and
a beer – so in that respect, it must have been odd suddenly to have
him as their boss. On the other hand, they were well aware of his
inventive brain, his ear for a room-stopping turn of phrase, the sheer
force of his personality, and for some, Brian Walker among them,
it was good to see him at last winning the recognition he deserved.

Brian had known him from the jazz clubs since the early Fifties,
and had been chronicling his exploits in his diary since 1955. Self-
effacing and living miles away from the jazz scene crowd at Hinton
Blewett, he was able to present himself as an enthusiastic amateur
rather than the skilled musician he was for the simple reason that he
had a considerable day job as a cartoonist and illustrator of national
repute. Born in Bristol in 1926, he trained at the West of England
College of Art after he left the RAF in 1947 and was soon having
cartoons published in Punch as well as working as a freelance writer
for *Picture Post, John Bull* and *Lilliput* among others. Just about
the time the Wurzels were taking off he was offered work by D C
Thomson, the *Beano* and *Dandy* publishers in Dundee, and early
in 1967 he found it no great trauma to leave the band of which, in
truth, he had always been a somewhat semi-detached member.

John Macey was next to go, with young Henry Davies (Davis)
stepping into his shoes. John had tried the full-time lark once before,

going to London with Acker Bilk, but had come back to Bristol and soon realised that even in a band based on home turf, this still wasn't the life for him. The summer of 1967 saw the pub landlord Reg Chant call time on his Wurzelry, and the band lose its foothold on his upstairs room for rehearsing. Temporary Wurzels including Pete Shutler of the Yetties stepped into the void until Tommy Banner was signed up in time for those glorious World Cider Drinking Championships in November that year. 'Adge knew Richie Bryant in Acker's band,' John Miles recalls. 'Richie knew Tommy up in Scotland and so, as Adge was forever telling the crowd, "I couldn't find a good accordionist in the West Country, so I went to Scotland to get a crap one." He called him Jock McSpreader and all kinds of things, but signing the Only Scottish Wurzel in Captivity turned out to be a good thing.'

Tommy remembers his first meeting with Adge, a couple of weeks before joining the band. Both of them were working in the North and Barnsley railway station seemed as good a place as anywhere, since the Wurzels were in cabaret in the town. It was at a place called the Ba Ba Club, owned by Peter Casson, a stage hypnotist whose gimmick was to have a dozen people wandering around the stage at the same time, all doing silly things. Oh, how the audience laughed. 'John Miles told me about this arrangement to meet up, and I asked how I'd know who to look for; I hadn't the faintest idea what this Adge Cutler looked like. "Oh, you'll recognise him," John said. But how can I? "You will." And I did.'

Movement within the band for the rest of Adge's time with it was minimal. When Henry Davies was tempted to go back to London in 1968 to join the New Vaudeville Band, Melt Kingston stepped in as bass player, even though he had never played string bass before. He soon learned, despite the fact that his first session with Adge, after being picked up at Temple Meads and taken to Nailsea, was liberally laced with scrumpy from Adge's parlour. It was the day he had to go to the press launch of the advertising campaign for Mr Brains Faggots, so Melt went along with him to be introduced to the press – and presumably the rest of the band. Melt told Frank Blades of the Wurzelmania website that yet more drink was consumed there, and the next day he woke up with a terrible hangover and vague memories of two Wurzels songs: 'Thus armed, he made his debut with the band that evening!'

Both he and Tommy Banner have identical tales of being taken by Adge to buy hats, both to rather staid and seemly shops and Melt, indeed, to Dunne's, then a very respectable gentlemen's outfitters a world away from Raselle's pawn shop on Old Market. 'Melt was paraded in front of Adge in his new gear,' Frank Blades wrote. 'Adge looked quizzical, took the nice new hat from Melt's head, threw it on the floor, jumped on it a couple of times and replaced it. "There, that's better!" he announced.' Tommy remembers the prim and proper shop assistant prinking up the hat with its dinky little feather before handing it to 'Sir', only to be mortified as Adge gave it the works.

Things did not work out well for Henry Davies in London, and with Melt Kingston heading back there – to take his place in the New Vaudeville Band, in fact – he went to Adge wondering if his old job was vacant again. It wasn't, since Tony Baylis had already replaced Melt, but what the Wurzels did need was a musical director for their next LP, *Cutler of the West*, and from his knowledge of Henry's abilities, Adge knew he would be just the man.

The Cutler-Quantrill-Banner-Baylis line-up stood firm until the last few months of Adge's life, give or take odd occasions when a variety of Bristol musos found themselves called to the colours.

At around the time of the Kingston-Baylis changeover another old mate from the local jazz scene, Peter Skuse, played a couple of gigs on string bass at the Portcullis in Chipping Sodbury. 'The band I was with, the Riverside Jazz Band, was appearing with them there, and when for some reason they needed somebody to dep, Adge asked me if I could sit in and do it,' he says. 'We'd bumped into each other previously at the Bell in Walcot Street, Bath, where the Riverside did most of its gigs. He'd come in just to listen to the music, and obviously thought I was up to scratch. I'm glad he did, because I still have happy memories of my time as a very temporary Wurzel. Later we met again after I'd gone full-time and was with the group playing at Ashton Court Country Club. Adge was there for a week in cabaret, and I remember him falling off a bar stool one night after his set. Was he drunk? I don't know. But he fell off his bar stool.'

Adge and Reg Quantrill had a love-hate relationship, on stage and off. Maybe that is too strong, and they simply did not like one another very much. Flamboyant Adge and deadpan Reg struck many as a classic comedy partnership, and the latter was well prepared for all the daft taunts that came his way – 'the man who puts the "sod" in Chipping Sodbury', ' the Engelbert 'Umperdinck of West 'Arptree', 'Snake 'ips Quantrill, the Elvis Presley of Chewton Mendip', that kind of thing.

'Adge was always trying to come up with bits of business that Reg didn't want to know about,' says Henry Davies. 'As Reg played both banjo and guitar, Adge thought it would be good for him to come on with them on either side of a yoke over his shoulders, but Reg, whose upper left arm had been shortened by TB, said that wouldn't look right. Then Adge wanted to put a little thatched roof on Reg's amp. He wouldn't have that, either, and when Adge wanted to get a comedy dialogue going between them, it never quite worked.

He wanted to do this routine: "You remind me of a character from Dickens." "Mr Pickwick?" "No, Uriah Heep," but Reg always tried to elaborate it, put in an extra line or phrase, and the timing would be ruined.'

Reg Quantrill, who died in the spring of 2012 aged seventy-seven, was a well loved figure on the Bristol jazz scene and one who in the early days was central to the Wurzels' musical direction, laying down the chords and generally helping to bring form to tunes that came into the rehearsal room buzzing around Adge's head. But he got off on the wrong foot with Tommy Banner when he seemed to imply that collecting pigswill was more important than going through the arrangements with his new band mate, and it got worse some time later when he failed to show for what the rest of the band saw as an important date. 'It was a press ball at the Mecca in Frogmore Street,' says Tommy. 'For some reason we'd been having a hard time from the Bristol newspapers, and we saw this as a real chance to build bridges. When Adge tackled him about it he said "I didn't think it was important."'

It was when, towards the end of 1973, various domestic issues in Reg's life began to further affect his reliability in turning up for dates that John Miles and Adge took the decision to replace him. They needed a professional used to full-time work, and with the Bristol jazz scene by no means the happy hunting ground it once was, they turned to Pete Budd, well known to the manager as the singer, guitarist and face of the Bristol group the Rebels. Come the mid-Seventies, the lads were beginning to look a bit long in the tooth for rebellion, and in truth even the young Pete had never been exactly James Dean, and there was something about him that made John think he could fit the part. 'I had known Pete Budd since 1960, with the Rebels, and if it hadn't been for him the Wurzels wouldn't have carried on,' he says today. The story about his call-up is well known: Reg could not do a gig in Weston-super-Mare, and Tommy Banner was sent out to search for Pete. He traced him to one of his fishing spots on the River Huntspill, and he answered the call.

'I went home and got ready, and I remember I had to wear Reg Quantrill's clothes,' he said. 'He was twice the size I was; in fact I was pretty skinny in those days. After the gig Adge asked me if I would like to join the Wurzels. I played the guitar, but Adge wanted the banjo. "You can get one o' they and learn to play 'ee," he told me. He didn't realise a guitar has six strings and a banjo just four, but after a week I mastered it.' It was after Adge's death when Pete was hastily drafted in as lead vocalist that he really came into his own, and with his authentic West Country accent and broad smile, he was a hit from the start. After May 1974, the Banner-Budd-Baylis line-up stayed together until Tony's departure in 1983, and of course it was this trio that made it big in 1976 with the huge hits *Combine Harvester* and *I Am A Cider Drinker*. A few Wurzels have come and gone since then, notably bassists, and Jai Howe (1983-1984 and 2002-2007), Terry Pascoe (1983-1984), Mike Gwilliam (1984-1995), Dave Wintour (1995-2002) and Louie Nicastro (2006) all did sterling service in the corduroys and neckerchiefs. Today, drum and bass are key to the contemporary sound of the band, in the able hands of John Morgan (since 1981) and Sedge Moore, a Wurzel since 2007. And Tommy and Pete? They're not saying they'll go on for ever, but they will while they're still enjoying it. And they're enjoying it.

Yvonne

Adge Cutler and Yvonne Tucker had known one another for years, from a distance. In the Fifties both had been regular faces on the Bristol jazz scene, usually in the crowd but sometimes up on stage, doing their numbers. The difference was that she was quite a singer, and though she'd happily belt out *Stormy Weather* or *Old Devil Moon* simply for the joy of doing it, she was good enough to get paid for her performances sometimes. Adge? Well, he was just Adge, wasn't he?

Both were big personalities, 'real characters'. Everybody says it of them, still. 'Adge? Oh, he was a real character.' 'Yvonne? Oh, she was a real character.' Each had their circle of friends, Yvonne's wider than Adge's and taking in much of bohemian Bristol, including the motley crowd at the art college, where she was a life model. They say life models don't have to be beautiful, that interesting faces and awkward bodies are just as welcome as classic good looks, but Yvonne was simply gorgeous, with a vivacious, outgoing personality to go with it.

She probably reminded her husband of women he'd seen in Spain. Later, after they had married, some folks in Nailsea took her to *be* Spanish, and if he had known that, he would have been delighted. But that doesn't mean he was about to walk up and ask her for a date, since as we have noted, there was a retiring side to Adge that melted away when he stood up to do his stuff and was obscured when he was surrounded by the likes of Dick Best and Spanish Mayne. But try chatting up Yvonne Tucker? Yvonne Tucker, divorced mother of several children? Yvonne Tucker, more than seven years older than him? Bit out of the league of a Nailsea boy, that one.

The many friends and acquaintances of Adge who have helped with this book have not held back in their accounts of him, warts and all. Remembered indiscretions abound, some of which have found their way into these pages, some not. What has been almost totally absent has been any reference to his relationship with women. 'He had a bit of an eye for the ladies, mind': none of that at all, not a breath of it. There would have been women, particularly in the world-wide travelling of the Acker Bilk years, but his preferred milieu was the crowd, with a buffer of old friends around him, most of whom really were there for the beer, the music, the craic. He knew some people in the crowd Yvonne knew, but he also knew when he was out of his comfort zone. In all probability, it never crossed his mind that she would be remotely interested in him.

Which just goes to show, for in an unpublished memoir written years after Adge's death, Yvonne Cutler admitted that she had 'always admired him from afar' at that time, doubtless attracted by the buzz he forever seemed to have around him, even though she played no part in it. As it was, it was not until his return from Spain in the mid-Sixties that they got together: 'I was a member of the Dug Out Club [in Park Row, where she also sang regularly] and it had strict rules – members only, guests to be signed in, formal dress compulsory. Thursday was jazz night, and it was one stormy Thursday evening, with a gale howling through the door and a queue of frozen, dripping people waiting to get in, that I spotted Adge. His friends hadn't arrived, so I signed him in, and after a warning from the doorman to wear a collar and tie in future he was admitted, under protest. Lots of our mutual friends were there and we spent an unforgettable evening, listening to the Blue Notes and eating chicken in a basket. He walked me home and over coffee, we agreed to meet again next day.'

Nellie Yvonne was born in Leicester on February 29, 1924 to Lizzie, the wife of Eugene Tanguay (some records have it as Tanquay), a French Canadian cobbler who chose to cross the Atlantic at the height of the Great Depression and spent some time in Ireland. It was a desperate childhood for Nellie, in which her mother had a severe breakdown when she was eight, and she spent the next eight or so years in an orphanage in Bristol. When she was old enough she buried that name forever and lived the rest of her life as Yvonne; or sometimes, when she was singing, as Lucy Bailey, a name familiar to Adge fans, as we note in Chapter 12. Her first job was with a tailor on Christmas Steps, Bristol, and her skills as a needlewoman never left her. Then, at nineteen, she married a big band musician called Ted Tucker, who was leading his own band in the city when she first met him in the Forties; a drummer adept at the accordion, he was also percussionist for the once formidable BAC band at Filton. They stayed together for some years, and Lawrence (Larry), Su, Carol and Bob followed, but the strains in their marriage eventually became intolerable and they parted. Life had not been easy for Yvonne, for all her bubbly ways.

Geraldine Box, a later regular in the Bristol jazz clubs, got to know her very well and was a model with her for many years at the art college, based at first at the Royal West of England Academy and from 1969 in its new home at Bower Ashton, close to that part of town where 'the cars go by like thunder, and up and round and under'. 'There were so many parties, arts balls and get-togethers my husband Keith and I still remember fondly, including one where Adge turned up as Friar Tuck,' says Geraldine. 'As for working with Yvonne, my best memory is one summer day when the two of us posed for a life class – with clothes on, "costumed" – lying in the sun drinking wine in the woods at Ashton Court. We both thought that was a pretty good way to earn a day's pay!'

When Yvonne met Adge it was at the time he was trying to make it as a folk singer in Bristol, living on next-to-nothing in the flat in Pembroke Road. Yvonne was in a flat just behind, in Buckingham Place, but she was not alone, since there was the not inconsiderable matter of her younger son, Bobby. 'I was nine or ten, and I didn't like this new man at all,' says Bob Tucker today. 'I thought he was a very gruff, rough, uncouth kind of bloke, but most of all I was jealous because Mum liked him. I was also worried, even at that age, that we had no money and suddenly she was feeding this extra mouth. We didn't have enough for ourselves. That's the truth of the matter. When the two of them first met it was her subsidising him. Some people don't understand that. All I know is that at the time, as a child, I didn't approve of him.'

And then Adge's fortunes changed, and Yvonne enjoyed that as much as he did. Probably more. She lapped up the camaraderie of showbiz, the rubbing shoulders with the stars, the swapping backstage jokes with Tommy Cooper and Ken Dodd and making Morecambe and Wise laugh when she thought – at the height of their fame – that they were called Wise and Morecambe. They thought that was cute. A lot of people thought Yvonne was cute. They left Pembroke Road and Buckingham Place behind and moved into a spacious, roomy flat on the other side of Whiteladies Road, near the BBC. 'That was the first good place we lived in, 21 Tyndall's Park Road,' Bob Tucker recalls. 'It had nice high ceilings and Mum took charge of its decoration and furnishing. She had an eye for that.'

Bob remembers Adge as a remote stepfather, never ungenerous financially, certainly never abusive, but almost entirely detached from the young boy, unable to disguise the fact that it was solely his mother he was interested in. 'He was distant, nonchalant, he didn't care, but I have to say he was never unwilling to spend money on me,' Bob says. 'He bought me a private education at Clarks College in Bristol, and even went along with my mother to meet the head. He gave me £20 to buy a bike at Dawson's on Whiteladies Road and then coughed up another three when it didn't cover the one I wanted, and he paid for me to go pony-trekking when they went off to Spain. He didn't want me there, and I don't blame him for that. He bought me a dog, a bit like a Jack Russell, called Buster, but he was theirs as much as mine. He was with Adge on TV, once, playing the part of his "old dog Spot" in *Ferry to Glastonbury*. I heard a chap in Nailsea once saying Adge was mean, and I'll never have that. Mind you, I heard another chap in Nailsea saying he was Adge Cutler's stepson, and I thought "that's funny, I don't feel we've met before".

'Anyone who knew him knew he could be introverted, happy to sit at home and read the paper quietly. He liked nothing better than settling down in front of the telly and eating a nice meal, Spanish style. He never took me out much. I remember him frightening the life out of me in that MG he was killed in, tearing down that dip to Abbots Leigh. There were those trips to the seaside in his old bus with Roy's family and just occasionally I would go out with them in the evening. They were always socialising. Adge was invited everywhere, and Mum liked that little bit of notoriety. I remember when I was about thirteen, they took me to the Little Theatre at the Colston Hall in Bristol, where they were putting on a production called *Bristol Fashion* and using Adge's *Virtute et Industrial* in it. Everybody was schmoozing round him and I said in a stage whisper "Excuse me, my mother's a well known one as well". He heard me, and he thought that was great. He gave my mother a diary every year, and from then on he dedicated it to "A well known one".'

Adge and Yvonne married at the Register Office in Ringwood in the New Forest in 1972, at about the time they moved into Craigie Knoll on Tickenham Hill. Dick Best was the eponymous best man, Adge was smart in collar and tie and a blue double-breasted blazer and Yvonne went for the hippy look with a floppy hat, flowery top and grey slacks. The two surviving post-wedding snapshots outside the dreary looking office were presumably taken by a stranger, since Dick is also in one picture.

Adge lost no time in introducing her to Spain, and she was delighted to find that many people in Guernica found him as fascinating as his British friends and followers did. He was well in with the local bigwigs but he equally loved being out and about at the Monday market, and Yvonne was impressed by the sheer number of people he knew. She also marvelled at the way he could understand the language, not just textbook speech but the little jokes muttered in thick dialect. How could a foreigner do that? Adge could.

He got to know a well known regional singer and comedian, a Northern Spanish Adge Cutler, called Chomin del Regato, and they had many a happy session together. Dave Cutler is convinced his brother was granted some kind of civic honour by the people of Guernica. 'Didn't they make Adge the King of the Town or something?' he asks. No trace of this can be found, but he was certainly a very popular man there. On one of their visits, Adge and Yvonne were told that back in the Sixties, when he was broke, scruffy and unshaven, some Guernicans had suspected he was one of the Great Train Robbers on the run, but he had certainly not picked up on this at the time. 'He was sympathetic towards Guernica because of the horrific treatment it received in the Spanish Civil War, but more than that, he was sympathetic towards it because of the kind way its people had treated him when he was struggling back in the Sixties,' says Bob Tucker.

Craigie Knoll was the homecoming Adge had dreamed of and he loved the garden, even though Bob's sister Su has an affectionate abiding image of him wheeling a glittering array of new tools around in a barrow and never troubling to stop to use them. Yvonne, with her dressmaking skills, set about bringing a woman's touch to what had been a very run-down property, and for Adge the project was to make the outside look as much like Guernica as he could.

Buster gave the couple a lot of laughs, especially in his role as guard dog; he would bark if he heard an unusual noise, and then run under the bed. 'I'm not saying that dog's daft,' Yvonne told friends, 'but when we gave him four ice cubes the other day, he ate one and buried the other three in the garden.' There were also cats, quite a lot of them at one time, when a little stray tortoiseshell they took in presented them with five kittens one morning, snuggling into bed with them to start to do the business. 'I thought Adge was going to have kittens himself, jumping out of bed shouting "What shall we do? What shall we do?"' Yvonne recalled. 'We slipped an old towel under her and put her in the wardrobe, where she delivered the rest of her litter. Buster pushed the door open, inspected the kittens, closed the door again with his nose and then stood guard outside it.'

This paints a harmonious picture, but in truth it was not all joy and peace. Even those who liked Yvonne admit she drank too much for her own good, and that gave those who decided they did not like her, of whom there were plenty in Nailsea, a stick to beat her with. The couple also used to argue, often in public and occasionally with flying drink and food, and this was of further concern for her friends and grist for her enemies' mill. Roy and Sheila Cutler have particularly unhappy memories of nights out at the Webbington and and Ashton Court, when Adge and Yvonne quarrelled bitterly. They could not have been good to be with at such times, and it is not surprising that some people began to draw conclusions about the state of their marriage.

'Oh, she was fiery all right, and they had some right good old barneys,' says Bob Tucker. 'But I know she loved him dearly, and they were well suited, they were good together. Would they still be together today? I think they would.' Geraldine Box also feels the two were well matched, while admitting that 'Yvonne must have been very expensive to keep. Drink was a problem for her.' Geraldine looks back with a shudder at the culture of the art college at Bower Ashton back then, when the bar was open from ten o' clock in the morning until midnight, and she remembers feeling relief in summer when the college was closed, and that particular temptation was taken away from her friend – and, in truth, a good many more at the college – for a couple of months. Most of all, though, her abiding memory of Yvonne is as a vibrant person, full of life and energy: 'She was so vivacious and beautiful, very dark. She talked about Adge as "my boy", with great affection. Yes, I'd have said they were well matched.'

'We thought Yvonne was smashing,' says Dave Cutler. 'Margot was great friends with her. OK, she used to drink a bit. I don't think it was that people around Nailsea didn't like her because suddenly she'd taken their old drinking buddy away from them. I don't think she changed his life very much at all in that respect! But she was quite a character, one of those people you either liked or you didn't. We did.' The same cannot be said for Roy and Sheila Cutler, whose antipathy towards her turned to something deeper after Adge's crash, and there was acrimony over the will.

As an average looking guy, one of his problems would be summed up to perfection some years after his death by that incisive philosopher Dr Hook in *When You're in Love with a Beautiful*

Woman: 'Everybody wants her, everybody loves her, Everybody wants to take your baby home...' Adge would be constantly seeking reassurance from their friends, making plain his fears. 'Were you with Yvonne on Tuesday?' he asked one of her women friends meaningfully.

In truth, anybody transplanted from the world Adge had met her in would have found it difficult to settle and be universally accepted in the Nailsea of the early Seventies. They were worlds he could straddle with ease, the contrasting cultures of small-town life and big-city bohemia which by this time had turned into showbiz and mateyness with the likes of Ken Dodd. In fact he had never had trouble compartmentalising his life in this way, right back to the early Fifties. You see pictures of him as a young man, his head full of rhymes, and he could only be a beatnik, or someone influenced by that culture, in his cool black jersey; yet contemporary photographs show him out for the night with his Nailsea buddies, all sharp in their narrow ties and pre-teddy boy Burton's suits, and he could not look more at home with them.

What it did all add up to is that when he was no longer there, it was an easy decision for Yvonne to sell up at Craigie Knoll, get back into town and leave all the endless wrangling over the will and the garage business and the sale of the vehicles and the rest to her solicitors. She parted with Craigie Knoll for nine thousand pounds more than its purchase price, not an astonishing profit considering the money that had been spent on it at that time of teeteringly high inflation, but the house she bought in Goldney Road, Clifton, was big enough to be let out as flats. Yvonne had just turned fifty when she was widowed, no age at all, but she did not remarry and while renewing many old friendships and acquaintanceships in the city, she knew life there would never be as crazy as it was in the Fifties and early Sixties; she had no wish for it to be, with Buster the dog and Um-row the cat from the Tickenham days still keeping her company in her early years back in town.

Health problems became an issue in her later years, and she died alone from a heart attack on February 14, 1999 – Valentine's day. It was just a few days short of her seventy-fifth birthday although she insisted, as leap year babies are privileged to do, that really she was still in her teens. 'Valentine's day,' her daughter Su muses. 'She'd have liked that, but it was all very sad. I'd fitted her up with an alarm, one of those bleepers vulnerable people wear round their necks, but of course she hadn't got it on. She died at night and was not found until lunchtime the next day, when friends she had arranged to meet grew concerned and went round to her flat to investigate.'

Yvonne's funeral was at All Saints Church in Pembroke Road, Clifton, and people from the Fifties Bristol scene who had not seen one another for years got together to remember one of their brightest. Afterwards, at the Polish Club in St Paul's Road, and later at the Combined Services Club near by, a lot of jazz was played, old memories were revived and word has it that even a glass or two was drunk. For her four Tucker children and some of their families, there was an equally touching little ceremony when they dedicated a bench in her memory on the edge of the Downs in Clifton, just across from Christ Church. 'We had a little party with balloons and champagne, and we sang Adge's old songs,' Bob Tucker remembers happily. 'We offered drinks to anyone who passed by, but I think they thought we were happy clappers from the church across the road, and they said no. What I remember most was when one of the balloons broke free from all the rest, and wafted away down the road in the direction of the pub. "Uh-oh," we said, "there she goes. That's Mum."

Sunday May 5, 1974

There was an end-of-term buzz about the Crystal Room after the show. Not only was it the last night of the week-long run, but the Wurzels were looking forward to their first days off for weeks on end. That was one reason they had travelled up separately that night; they all had different agendas after they left Hereford. Almost at the last minute Adge had decided to do the trip alone in his newly-repaired MGB, after at first arranging to be driven by the new boy in the band, Pete Budd. He loved the drive up the Wye Valley, and there was never a better time of year to see it than in early May, with Tintern Abbey nestling against its green backdrop and white blossom in the hedgerows.

Come half past midnight, most of the boys were away: Pete welcomed the chance to go straight home, without the detour via Tickenham Hill; Tony Baylis had a long journey back home to London ahead of him – what would be the best way from here? – and Tommy Banner, who was living in Easton-in-Gordano at the time, had some serious football business to attend to. He was not surprised to see that Adge would be the last to leave. As a band leader – as a sombre document soon to be drawn up would describe him – he had matters both social and commercial to attend to with the club management; to reduce it to strictly business terms, leaving all sentiment aside, he wanted the group's money for the week and he wanted to cement the kind of relationship that ensured the Wurzels would always be welcomed back with open arms. He had no cause for concern on either front at the Crystal Room.

'I was away by about half past midnight, and was looking forward to the break,' says Tommy Banner. 'The last I saw of Adge he was talking with Aiden J Harvey, and as always he seemed to be enjoying his company.' In fact for Adge it was stacking up to be anything but a Wurzels-free Sunday for later that day, after a few hours' sleep, he was due to meet up with John Miles to discuss a possible TV series in Canada and other promising leads. By this stage in his career he was far from starry-eyed: for every appearance on peaktime TV he knew there was likely to be weeks of slogging around the cabaret circuit, and if every date turned out to be as congenial and friendly as the Crystal Room, that would be a bonus. But his manager had sounded genuinely excited about these new developments, Canada had already shown a liking for his work, and he wanted to know more. It could just be the international breakthrough they had been waiting for for years.

It was 4.10am when Michael Kelly, a 25-year-old quantity surveyor, was leaving the eastbound M4 at the Newhouse roundabout, just a couple of minutes from his home in Bulwark, Chepstow; now junction 2 of the M48, this is the exit immediately beyond the original Severn Bridge and Wye Bridge for visitors from England. Mr Kelly had left the roundabout and was just beginning to head up the long, straight Wye Valley Link Road, the A466, when he saw a white sports car coming in the opposite direction. It looked to be being driven normally at an unexceptional kind of speed, maybe thirty or forty mph, and doubtless the only reason he noticed it at all was that he was a young man with an eye for a sporty car – his own was a Ford Capri – and after all, there was little else to look at on the road at that time of morning. In those days the A466 at this point was a three-carriageway two-way road, so oncoming traffic was considerably closer to hand than it is today.

'I fancy I noticed the driver sitting upright in his seat,' he told the police later that day. 'As [the car] passed me I heard the engine rev, as if the driver was changing gear. My offside window was open, and just after the sports car passed me I heard a squeal of brakes, and a squeal of skidding tyres.'

Adge's car had hit a triangular grass traffic island as the A466 reached the Newhouse roundabout. Brake marks on the road showed that instead of following the curve of the road leftwards on to the roundabout, the MG had continued straight over the corner of the triangle, taking a No Entry sign with it. It then crossed the roundabout road, hitting the kerb hard on the other side, and then lost its windscreen as it careered into a low rock outcrop in the grass roundabout verge. Mr Kelly watched all this in horror, noting that all the time the brake lights were on until impact with the rock sent the car hurtling towards the left and turning over three or four times until it landed on its wheels facing towards Chepstow, in the opposite way from which it had been coming.

'I went to the scene and saw... its headlights were on full beam and engine still running,' his witness statement continued. 'I found the driver trapped underneath the rear nearside wheel, face downwards... I switched the engine off for safety's sake. I tried to push the car away from the driver, but the front nearside tyre was completely flat and almost off the rim, and I failed to move it. Other people came, and went for the police and ambulance.'

Mr Kelly added that he tried to assist further, 'but there was nothing I could do. I think he was still alive at that time. The police later arrived... and the car was lifted off him and he was taken to hospital in the ambulance'.

PC David Jones testified that he reached the scene at 4.30am and that 'lying face downwards with his hands and arms above his head was the body of a man. The near rearside wheel was resting on the back of his head and left hand. With assistance, the car was lifted forward and he was released. He appeared to be dead...' The weather was fine, clear and dry, and the high-level multi-lights on the roundabout made for good visibility. The time of Adge's death is recorded as 5am, when he was pronounced dead on arrival at the Royal Gwent Hospital in Newport.

It was 7.30am when the police rang John Miles with the dreadful news, and he was immediately in touch with Adge's family. It was 8am when he contacted Tommy Banner, a little later when he got through to Tony Baylis and the unusual reaction of both of them, woken up after a very late night, was identical. Each of them answered the phone, heard the message, instantly went back to sleep and then woke up in panic. That was just a dream, a nightmare – wasn't it? How they wished that it was. Pete Budd did not hear the sad tidings before he got to the pub for a Sunday lunchtime pint and game of darts. 'Didn't think we'd see you in here today...' His was probably the cruellest experience of all. 'It was so sudden, we didn't know what to do,' he said later. 'It was like losing a brother.' Pete's first concern after taking in the news was to contact his father, who still thought his son had been taking Adge up to Hereford that night.

There was business to be done in Gwent that morning, unpleasant business, and while it fell to Roy Cutler, the elder of the surviving brothers, to identify the body, he was accompanied by John Miles and his brother Dave.

'First I heard of it was that morning, when the phone was ringing and it was my brother Roy,' says Dave Cutler. 'He said "Adge has been involved in a fatal accident" and all I could say was is he all right? How stupid was that?' In fact it was not remotely stupid. Roy, in an attempt to spare his kid brother's feelings, had left out the only piece of information that mattered. Almost immediately, John Miles was on the phone to Dave. Then it was Adge's wife, Yvonne, asking him to identify the body: 'She'd phoned us because she and Roy's wife Shirley didn't get on very well, whereas Margot and I liked her.' In fact it was Roy who formally identified Adge as the victim, at 11.45am, although all three were present in the mortuary at St Woolos Hospital, Newport.

'First of all, for some reason, we went to look at the car at the police station in Chepstow,' Dave remembers. 'They'd looked at it and all they'd found wrong with it was a broken brake disc, which had obviously been caused by the impact at the roundabout.' Roy Cutler had serviced the car only a couple of days previously, and was anxious that no claim of negligence should be laid at his door, but of course that was never a serious proposition. Roy, incidentally, has no memory of the earlier accident noted in Chapter 1 of this book, in which the MGB was damaged in an accident on the M4 near Swindon after Adge had apparently fallen asleep at the wheel. Nevertheless, both John Tucker and Tommy Banner, who were with him separately on that final Saturday, are certain they are not mistaken.

Roy Cutler remembers: 'We got to the police station in Chepstow and met up with the policeman who had found him, who was almost dead on his feet at this stage. His eyes were pretty well drooping down on his chest. Then we went over to Newport to identify the body, and after we'd found somebody to open up the morgue, they let us in. You couldn't see any damage on him, and he was lying there with a silly little smile on his face. We're a forthright family, and all I could say was well, Adge, you've done some damn silly things in your life, but you've never done anything as daft as this before.'

The Wurzels got together with their manager on the Monday, all three of them convinced it was the end of the line. How could it possibly not be? Adge was the face of the band, the spokesman, the front man, the star. Apart from that, after this devastating blow, who in their right mind would want to go on? 'That Sunday morning, all of them said it was all over,' says John Miles. 'I said look, the press are going to ring me any minute and you can't say you're not going to go on and then change your mind. I'm going to say that you *are* going to go on, and then we'll talk about it later. They said "Oh, we can't really do that". I said come on, it'll keep Adge's songs alive. I'm going to say you're going to keep on performing for that reason. They were really against it, but I said I promise you, I'll get you a Number One record if you carry on. Why I said it I'm not sure. Desperation, I suppose. But of course the press did ring me, and the following day it was big news.'

The two big Bristol newspapers, while under the same ownership, worked separately and on different time scales in those days. The morning *Western Daily Press* gave a straight report on the crash and the shocked reaction to it, but come the afternoon, the *Evening Post* was already carrying the story forward with 'King Adge dies in crash, but... WE'LL PLAY ON, SAY THE WURZELS'. The story was the page three lead, with a blurred three-column photograph of the car, looking not unduly damaged, and an even more blurred single-column head-and-shoulders block of Adge. The page one lead was a story raking over the former Home Secretary Reginald Maudling's links with the by now disgraced architect John Poulson. Regional press news values would be different these days.

Tommy Banner and Pete Budd agree that persuasive though their manager could be and was, it was the public who really forced the Wurzels' hand. 'We kept getting calls from people asking if we would be fulfilling booked gigs, so we thought we'd give it a try and get an act together,' said Pete. 'It turned out to be such a success that we decided to keep it going. Adge was such a character that there was no way to replace him, so we had to carry on as we were and do something a little different.'

'Yes, it was the people who'd booked us who railroaded us to go on,' Tommy agrees. 'On that Monday morning, the phone never stopped ringing. You must keep going, they were saying. We decided to take a month off, but in the end it was just two weeks before we were on the road again, with a gig organised in Bayton, Worcestershire by the village's musician postmaster Brian Link.'

Brian Turner, the manager of the Crystal Room, told the press that Adge had appeared at the club before, but this was the first time the Wurzels had been around for a full week of cabaret: 'Last week was a real sell-out. I didn't realise Adge intended to travel back home. Very often we arrange hotels in Hereford for artists, but as far as I can gather the rest of the group made their own arrangements.' The club owner, Desmond Macquire, said: 'Adge had been playing here all week, and I think he had been driving home every night. Although he sang about the cider, he didn't strike me as a drinking man. Off stage he was very quiet – but his shows went like a bomb here.' One of his staff, Pearl Morgan, added: 'It had been a very good evening. The place was absolutely packed. Adge and the group stopped behind to talk to staff and customers, and everyone was in good spirits.'

In his recorded interview with Mel Gordon, 'Drink Up Thy Zider' George Rollings said: 'It was terrible when he died. I couldn't believe it. I knew he didn't drink and I knew that though his car was a sports car, he wasn't a bloke to go tearing around. The whole family was in shock. The whole village. Is it true? Have you heard anything? Is he in hospital? I didn't know. I had a ganger man's job, and this bloke come up and said "'Ere, you know about Cutler?" I said no, what's that then? He said he was killed coming home from

South Wales, I think he said. I sat down on a heap of bricks and I just couldn't get up again. I was absolutely stunned. All of the blokes around knew him. It was the sort of thing where you wanted to send everybody home for the day. Everyone was in absolute shock.'

Shock, and tears. There were plenty of those at the Orange Tree pub in Hereford, where Adge had been laughing and joking with them only hours before. 'We heard the terrible news at about eleven o'clock that morning,' says Philip Morris. 'One of our regular customers was a retired police officer, a village bobby, and he had picked it up on the police grapevine. Jacko's daughters Anne and Jackie cried their eyes out. We were all just speechless.' It was also an ex-policeman who broke the news to Adge's old architect friend Ted Cowell, who was living in Devon preparing for a society barn dance starring the Wurzels: 'My wife Molly and I were at some friends' farmhouse, making plans for two of the boys to stay the night there. Then one of their friends, a former police officer, burst in, and said "Have you heard about Adge Cutler?" Molly just burst into tears.'

The week at the Crystal Room had been booked by Howard Rudman's Tower Agency in Fairfax Street, Bristol, and he is one of many of Adge's associates who have played that night over and over again in their minds. 'He was a tight old so-and-so moneywise,' he says. 'You couldn't blame him. He'd had it hard. I told him to stay up there, not to be dashing home in the middle of the night. He could have got a little B&B for peanuts. But for whatever reason, he wanted to come home. It wasn't drink that killed him. That's a bad road down the Wye Valley, it would soon have found him out if he had been drunk. It was just tiredness.'

Adge's old Portbury B workmate Hector Hook is another who regrets that Adge had not handled that night differently. 'I wish that like a lot of people who had done well, he had not ignored the decision to employ a good, reliable teetotal driver to be at his beck and call at times like that,' he says. 'Leslie Crowther, Dickie Valentine... But when you think about it, he'd driven all the way down the Wye Valley from Monmouth that night, all those twists and turns, the ninety degree corners at the bridge at Bigsweir, and if you'd really had too much to drink, you'd have come to grief long before the motorway roundabout.'

Adge's tragedy put many people in mind of the Fifties crooner Dickie Valentine's death three years earlier almost to the day; almost to the hour, in fact, since he crashed at 4.20am on May 6, 1971, again in South Wales, on a single-lane bridge at Glangrwyney, near Crickhowell. Aged a year younger than Adge at forty-one, he too was returning home after a club date, at the Double Diamond in Caerphilly, but here the similarities end: Dickie was tearing along at ninety miles an hour, and the accident also took the lives of his pianist and drummer.

The comedian Leslie Crowther survived when his Rolls Royce hit the M5 central reservation near Cheltenham after he had fallen asleep at the wheel on his way home from a show, but his injuries brought an end to his career and hastened his death.

'Adge was very sensible about driving, because so many people in our job have had accidents through tiredness,' John Miles told the *Western Daily Press*. 'If he felt tired he would always stop and have a few hours' sleep at the roadside.' Maybe he even snatched forty winks somewhere along the Wye Valley; after all, the Crystal Room was little more than an hour's drive away from the Newhouse roundabout. What John doubtless had in mind when he made that statement was an incident some time previously when the band had been playing a summer season of Tuesday nights at a holiday park in Croyde Bay, North Devon.

'Adge always wanted to get home, while the rest of us loved to stay the night there and enjoy the holiday atmosphere,' says Tommy Banner. 'In the morning we'd get up not particularly early, stop at a transport café at South Moulton and then head on north up the A38. One day at around mid-day, maybe even one o'clock, we were driving past a layby near Taunton and spotted him fast asleep in his car in a layby. There was not a lot of talk about sleep apnea or narcolepsy in those days, but I honestly wonder whether that was what he had.'

The cremation was at South Bristol Crematorium and Cemetery at Bedminster Down on the afternoon of May 24. It was supposed to be a private affair, and the city's two newspapers respected the family's wishes and did not report on it. In fact all there was in the *Evening Post* about him that evening was an advertisement for Adge Cutler's Wurzels appearing with Fred Wedlock at the South West 18-Plus dance at Bath Pavilion on Saturday June 1, tickets 95p. Still, the small funeral party was surprised – and in truth, probably far more heartened than hurt – when they found people lining the road and thronging around the cemetery gates, considerably more than a thousand strong. Their journey had begun in Nailsea, where the hearse had been driven slowly around the town to allow the people, Adge's people, to pay their last respects, but they had not foreseen such a spontaneous outpouring of affection in the city. 'A very prominent music publisher was there, and when he came back to my house afterwards he told me he had been amazed to see all those people,' says John Miles. 'He'd very recently been to the big band leader Eric Winstone's funeral [he died three days before Adge] and there had been just a dozen people there.' 'Band leader' it said on his death certificate, and this was a desperate time for members of that profession, Messrs Cutler and Winstone aside. Geraldo had died on the same weekend as Adge, who was buried on the day of Duke Ellington's passing.

Shortly afterwards, the burial of his ashes in Christ Church graveyard in Nailsea ended in a wake at the Royal Oak, where the Wurzels played at the site of the first great get-together that had launched them to fame, and Roy Cutler sang a few numbers with them. Indeed, he appeared with them at gigs once or twice after that, including a rugby club evening near Bath, but nothing permanent came of it, and none of those concerned expected it to. 'He's got a better voice than Adge had,' says Roy's wife Sheila. Yes, and so have a lot of other people. But they aren't Adge, are they?

At a coroner's inquest at Newport Civic Centre on June 28, seven good men and true heard the evidence of the hapless bypasser Mr Kelly and PC Thomas. They also heard the consultant pathologist who carried out the post-mortem, Geoffrey Andrews, say that the cause of death was cerebral laceration and haemorrhage caused by a skull fracture some seven inches long. The blood-alcohol reading was 157 milligrammes of alcohol in one hundred millilitres of blood, compared with the legal limit of eighty milligrammes: 'This is equivalent to just over five pints of beer or eleven single whiskies.'

The coroner, Glyn Evans, then made a statement to the jury that would raise eyebrows today and indeed did then among road safety campaigners. 'It does not indicate in my mind, despite what the law may say, that he was affected by drink so that he could not drive properly. He was over the legal limit, and he was committing an offence, but I don't think you need take any notice of the amount of drink he had taken. We are never going to know what caused him to continue straight on as he appears to have done. At this hour of the morning one does become sleepy and tired. One's attention is distracted. One does mistake lights at roundabouts.'

The jury returned a verdict of accidental death.

And so it was, but the war of words continued for some time afterwards. Barbara Castle's temerity in introducing the breathalyser in the late Sixties had enraged what would now be seen as the *Top Gear* constituency – she a *Labour* Transport Minister, she a *woman*, she a *non-driver* – and those who chose to interpret the coroner's words as a veiled attack on the law as it stood were very quick to do so. Their opponents, on the other hand, felt it questionable of Glyn Evans to appear to blame all of Adge's fatigue on the lateness of the hour, and none at all on the fact that the amount of alcohol in his blood was all but twice the legal limit.

The *Bristol Evening Post*'s headline on its report on the proceedings, 'Ignore amount he drank, Adge's inquest told' contributed to the widespread belief still held in the West Country that alcohol played little or no part in his death – and the *Post*, after all, was simply reflecting the thrust of the coroner's message. Interestingly, the two South Wales newspapers most concerned with the case, the *Western Mail* and the *South Wales Argus*, were rather more reluctant to take Glyn Evans's conclusion at face value. 'Singer killed in crash had been drinking', the *Mail* reported, 'Adge Cutler drank more than limit', the *Argus*.

There also seems to have been no discussion at the inquest on whether Adge would have fared better if he had been wearing his seat belt. Before leaving office in 1968 Mrs Castle had seen through a law to introduce these to all new cars, and Adge's 1971-72 MG was certainly fitted with them. Since it was not made compulsory for drivers and front seat passengers to use them until early 1983 – at the eleventh Parliamentary attempt to do so – Adge was well within his legal rights to choose not to do so, but some kind of consideration of their pros and cons might have been helpful. This particular case, in fact, was probably one of the minority in which it was better not to be belted up and trapped in a car with no roof protection as it rolled over three or four times. As it was, Adge was thrown out, and it was his grotesque misfortune for his head to end up exactly where the rear nearside wheel of his car came down on him. Heartbreakingly perversely, apart from his severe head injuries, there was scarcely a scratch on him: 'minor abrasions on the inside of the back of the left knee...' 'There is some brusing of the right hand...' That was about it. Otherwise he was a fit and healthy 'well nourished man', and if he had landed a yard to the right it would have been just another lucky escape to joke with the lads about while secretly worrying about what on earth was happening to him.

Today, all who knew Adge are convinced he fell asleep at the wheel once more, and woke up as soon as his car hit the green triangle at the junction: the racing of the engine was almost certainly not caused by him changing gear, and there was no question of his being 'confused by lights' as the first he knew of them was when he was almost on top of them.

As an aside, for people who set store by official documents in researching their family tree the inquest papers make unsettling reading, since they are riddled with errors. The death certificate records Adge's age as forty-three rather than forty-two; his house name, Cragie Knoll, taken from a braw Scottish landmark, is rendered as a resolutely Welsh Craig-y-Nowell on the post-mortem report; Nailsea is Nailsby on the police report to the coroner; and endearingly, it looks as if Yvonne lopped a leap year off her age when Roy Cutler asked her for it for his statement to the court. He gives it as February 29, 1928; four years earlier is the right one. And all of this in 1974, not 1774. The documents also give an interesting insight into the way in which words can be put into witnesses' mouths. In his statement the first man on the scene, Michael Kelly, said the police arrived 'later'; in some helpful constable's hand appears the insertion 'five to ten minutes', and although he must have thought they were the longest five minutes of his life, Mr Kelly signed the paper. In fact PC Thomas, who was not the one who took the statement, was perfectly up-front in recording the time of his arrival as 4.30am, some twenty minutes after the crash. That would not have been unusual in those days before mobile phones.

One or two mysteries and misapprehensions still surround that night, beginning with a widespread belief that if the car had been lifted from Adge more quickly, he would have survived. Since he died from impact injuries, that theory does not hold water.

Then there were the two policemen in a patrol car at the Highbeech roundabout, a mile back along the road, who said he had waved to them as he had driven past. They could be significant, as he was maybe from experience expecting to see them there, and his success in negotiating them might well have brought on a sense of comfortable well-being in him; another hurdle cleared. There was also, of course, the prospect of leaving Wales, where he had often found the audiences sticky, and getting back across that bridge. Not that there was not still work to do. Today's AA Route Planner shows the distance between the roundabout and Tickenham Hill as twenty-two miles, with a journey time of thirty-five minutes, but that was not the case on May 5, 1974. It *was* so from May 23 onwards – the day before Adge's funeral – because that was when the M5 Avon Bridge opened, taking fourteen miles and at least half an hour off the journey across the river. 'Oh, he was looking forward so much to that bridge opening, he was on about it all the time,' Tommy Banner recalls.

And finally, some people in Hereford swear that Adge's last appearance was not at the Crystal Room at all, but at an Eardisley Young Farmers' barn dance at Yew Tree Farm, Letton, in the heart of cider apple country twelve miles west of the city. They are totally convinced, while conceding that maybe he played at the cabaret club that night, too, but Tommy will have none of it. 'I'm afraid we hear this quite a lot,' he muses. 'The number of venues we did on the night he died is quite remarkable.'

Our Adge Top Ten

The Wurzels' songbook now extends to well over a hundred numbers, from vintage American rock 'n' roll to music hall, traditional and modern folk to punk and rap – much of it with tongue firmly in cheek, of course. But it all started off with Adge Cutler and the rhymes he dreamed up on the building site at Portishead, or cobbled together on the backs of cigarette packets in the pubs of Pill or the Gordano villages and neatly transcribed in school exercise books on the kitchen table back home behind his father's shop in Nailsea.

Adge's songs add up to around thirty in number: *All Over Mendip, Aloha Severn Beach, Avonmouth Mary, Barcelona Blues, The Champion Dung Spreader, Chew Magna Cha-Cha, Chitterling, Down in Nempnett Thrubwell* (with *Henry Davis*), *Drink Up Thy Zider, Easton-in-Gordano, Faggots is the Stuff, Ferry To Glastonbury* (with Colin Thomas), *Hark at 'Ee, Jacko, I'm the Captain of a Dredger* (with Henry Davis), *In the Haymaking Time, Look at 'Ee, Lookin' at I* (with Henry Davis), *Mabel, Mabel, The Mixer Man's Lament, Moonlight on the Malago, Pill, Pill, The Shepton Mallet Matador, The Somerset Space Race, Tanglefoot Twitch, Thee Cassn't Kill Cooch, Thee's Gott'n Where Thee Cassn't Back'n, Hassn't?, Twice Daily, Up The Clump, Virtute et Industrial* and *When the Common Market Comes to Stanton Drew,* along with joint credit with the rest of the Wurzels for *Willie The Shake,* the *Lily The Pink* parody on the *Carry On Cutler* album.

Market Gardener is another song credited to Adge and Henry Davis, but Tommy Banner believes it is the work of Bob Barratt and Tony Baylis. It is amusing to read sometimes that it was 'inspired by Adge's time as a market gardener', whereas it is just one long farrago of *double entendre*, all giant marrows and ladies' strawberry patches. *Don't Tell I Tell 'Ee* is credited to Adge as well as Kevin Sheldon and Trevor Crozier on the single, but not on any of the albums.

For this chapter we took a straw poll of the ten best-loved songs written and performed by Adge. It is likely that readers will agree with some of them, but as even our small poll exposed some quite sharp differences of opinion, we do not suppose that too many of you will be one hundred per cent at one with this list. Never mind. So here we go, in ascending order:

10, Twice Daily

Most in our poll placed it higher, but the author dislikes it so much that to include it at all represents a degree of compromise on his part. This, of course, was the one banned by the BBC, and it is accepted form to shrug one's shoulders and wonder what the silly old fuddy-duddies were on about. Lapsing into the first person for this paragraph only, I assume it is nothing to do with the bleeped-out 'bugger' or 'bleeder' but the unpleasant tone the song takes at the end of the second verse and into the third. There is something crude and violent in the way that 'zummat rips' on – or maybe in, as it is not made plain – the hitherto sweet and pure Lucy, and the young girl apparently being despatched by her lover to the doctor's possibly for some kind of (unsuccessful) abortion remedy hardly seems to be the stuff of comedy. The rhyming in the song is lazy – all those 'gailys' – and while this had no bearing on the BBC banning it, it strengthens my opinion that by doing so they did not deprive the listening public of very much. Ironically, *Twice Daily* is one of Adge's songs most recorded by other artists, with versions by the Irish 'JCB Man' Seamus Moore and two Canadian acts, Harry Hibbs and Shanneyganock, both of whom seem to have come to it via

Moore and have assumed it was an Irish song. All three sing it more quickly than Adge, take out the reference to the doctor, and have Lucy's garter slipping rather than zummat ripping. Best thing about Adge's version: the nice little in-joke with his wife Yvonne, who sang under the name of Lucy Bailey and owned with him a dog called Buster. The worst thing: everything else. Sorry folks. Sorry Adge.

9, Thee Cassn't Kill Cooch
Rather a touching song about a gardener's constant battle with the dreaded couch grass – touching in that it was composed at a time when Adge presumably thought he could go through his career writing folksy little tales of rural life. This is a song that portrays nature as some horrible monster to be slain – the kind of dragon that sees off St George every time.

8, Thee's Got'n Where Thee Cassn't Back'n, Hassn't?
The salutary story of Joe and Flo, who get into all kinds of predicaments driving their little car around Bristol and Paris, and poor Joe is forever getting it stuck in tight places where it won't come out. When Adge sang it to Fred Wedlock in the HTV car park after a show, Fred said straight away that he wanted to record it, and did. Suggestive? This is the Adge song that makes Eartha Kitt sound like Julie Andrews.

7, The Shepton Mallet Matador
How are they going to keep Jacko down on the farm after he's seen the Costas? This is the theme of this epic, for which the post-Adge Wurzels produced a funny video at what looks like five o'clock one sunny morning in Shepton Mallet centre. There sounds something autobiographical about:

Now the boys in the village all think it's very queer,
The way that Jacko drinks wine instead of beer...

and plenty of comic mileage in the lad waving his old red flannel shirt at the old red cow, and having the hens lay omelettes rather than eggs when he clicks his castanets. A knockabout song in itself, it has extra spice with that pinch of self-parody.

6, The Champion Dung Spreader

One that's still in the Wurzels' repertoire, and the song that launched the great Muck Spreading World Championships of 1969. The first lines make it clear that it's an answer to Lonnie Donegan's *My Old Man's a Dustman*, and there's something distinctly Doneganesque about:

Now many years ago, when Dad was in 'is power,
With a mighty two-hand swipe he hit the old church tower!
'Lord help us,' cried the vicar, 'Tis the judgement come!'
'Not so,' said the verger, 'Tis a hundredweight of dung!'

You can almost hear Lonnie in those last two lines, with the vicar's posh voice and the verger's down-beat reply, while *We'd all look out the way when they girt brown lumps go sailin'* is another classic Cutler line.

5, All Over Mendip

Another great one for the pub, a rollicking, drink up thy zider, rolling about kind of song that was put out by Columbia as the band's fourth single in 1967. An upbeat tale of a celebration to which all the surrounding villages in the hills are invited, it is still on the Wurzels' play list today. Reg Quantrill used to tell friends that the title stemmed from one night when he and Adge were driving to a gig and for some reason traffic seemed to be coming from all directions. 'Blimey, Reg,' Adge grumbled. 'They're all over Mendip tonight.'

4, Pill, Pill

Jazzy with a hint of sea shanty and a strong melody, this is Adge's worthy tribute to the community he saw as his second home.

> *When the nights are dark and stormy*
> *And the bitter north wind blows*
> *'Cross the fields from Shirehampton*
> *Where the muddy Avon flows...*

Must be as satisfactory a scene setter as any song could have, and the local lore comes in thick and fast as Adge touches on everything and everybody from the Pillites on the ferry to the warm, cosy and happy 'cobblers, hobblers and hobbledehoys' in the Duke [of Cornwall] and the Star. His mates at the King's Head must have wondered what they'd done wrong, but they were surely the only ones who didn't take to this song with open arms.

3, Virtute et Industrial

Adge's ironic song of affection for the far from virtuous and industrious backstreet people of Bristol and scathing scorn for the city fathers is surely his most quoted piece of work today, even though *Drink Up Thy Zider* is the most sung. Perhaps we must qualify 'most quoted'. It is the most quoted as his sharpest and most relevant social comment. In fairness, the funny rhymes of *When The Common Market Comes To Stanton Drew* are equally well remembered, but are never repeated with the passion thousands of Bristolians still bestow on Adge's famous lines:

> *With one-way streets and flyovers, who knows which way we'm facin'?*
> *Hast seen our brand new bridge, up there in Cumberland Basin?*
> *The cars go by like thunder, and up and round and under,*
> *Where they goes no bugger knows, an' 'tain't no bleedin' wonder!*

This is the song in which Adge has most fun with the local accent, from the Bristol 'L' on the end of the Latin motto that used to adorn the crest on the side of the city buses to the gloriously Bedminster:

> *Now we be Bristol kiddays, we comes from Bristol citay,*
> *Where all the boys be 'andsome, and all the girls be prettay...*

City, Rovers, talk of new docks at Portbury, a fear of the Welsh taking over – where did that one go? – the Concorde contract in the balance, the fact that:

> *From Lulsgate thees can tear off to Paris now by air,*
> *But the buses down Old Market street's enough to make thee swear...*

All this is set against a cast of characters standing up against the Establishment, getting by on the dole, shirking work, boozing and living on the never-never, and stripping aside its *Knees Up Mother Brown* bounciness this is work that stands up as pure protest poetry, performance poetry. Fred Wedlock recorded a version of it, which is praise enough – but if it had been written about Liverpool in the Sixties by Brian Patten or Adrian Henri it would now be in every anthology of Twentieth century verse.

2, When the Common Market Comes to Stanton Drew

This is the one for clever rhymes, daft analogies, complete mastery of metre, irony, sense of the ridiculous, erudition, even. This is the one that makes this writer so mad with Adge for slipshod tosh like *Twice Daily*. There's the prospect of the Eiffel Tower on 'Arptree 'Ill and gondolas down on the River Chew as we:

> ... *take the chance with Germany and France,*
> *And live like all they foreign people do.*

The tank of Portuguese vin blanc jammed up Pensford High Street will be another hazard as we look ahead to the time when:

> ... *we'll all drink caviar from a girt big cider jar,*
> *When the Common Market comes to Stanton Drew.*

The bars jammed to the doors with Messieurs and Senors, Timsbury full of Belgians and Radstock full of Dutch, all they foreign blokes with their girt big 'ats and cloaks chatting up the wenches on the village green with their *Ooh la la, oui oui* instead of 'How's bist thee?' What a picture Adge paints of our future in Europe, and if anyone you know still doubts the man's sheer talent and panache, just stick this verse under their nose:

> *Now as for what we eat, we must export more meat,*

Send 'em all our best prime beef and ham,
While we does stuff our guts with Transylvanian nuts
And garlic-flavoured processed German spam.
When George comes home from milkin', he'll get a big surprise,
When 'e sits down expectin' Irish stew,
And 'is wife says 'George, I'll get 'ee, a girt dollop of spaghetti',
When the Common Market comes to Stanton Drew.

The Wurzels' Tommy Banner must have heard that verse thousands of times, but it still creases him up. *'George, I'll get 'ee, a girt dollop of spaghetti,'* he muses. 'Nobody but Adge could have written that line, you know. Nobody.'

1, Drink Up Thy Zider

A song with three short, simple verses and as many choruses as you've got the lungs for, this is the national anthem of Somerset and Bristol, the song they roar at Ashton Gate, the one the Wurzels can't go on stage without playing, and save up for their third, lengthy encore. A lot of people still believe it's a traditional folk song and they can hardly be blamed, because every phrase of the chorus has a familiar ring about it:

Drink up thy zider...
For tonight we'll merry be...
We'll roll 'em in the clover...

Even the pay-off about the corn being half cut and so be we is unlikely to be an Adge original, but he and his first band put all the parts together in a way that made them fresh, and cheering, and full of the feelgood factor. The words are not remotely as ingenious as those of *Virtute* or *Stanton Drew*, but they skip along and there's a little bonus for West Country listeners in the line about going to see brother Ernie in Barrow Gurney. While the rest of the land simply hears another of Adge's folksy double-barrelled place names, those on his wavelength believe they detect something else in the air.

And what about: *There ain't nothin' like good zider for to make your smile grow wider*? So simple, so punchy, so completely the work of a lyricist at the peak of his form.

Bubbling under: *Ferry to Glastonbury, Chitterling, The Somerset Space Race* and *Easton-in-Gordano*. Fancy *Ferry to Glastonbury* having to make way for *Twice Daily*. Makes you weep, doesn't it?

Adge's Legacy

Adge's greatest legacy is surely the Wurzels themselves, still going strong after forty-six years and packing out venues still, wherever they go. Not that those venues are as numerous as they were, and nowadays they are almost exclusively, though not quite, restricted to the wider West Country. Much of their focus today is on the high summer months of June to August, and in 2012, if those three months can be described as high summer, they did thirty-five riotous shows. Some of those gigs in particular would have gladdened Adge's heart – Portishead Carnival, the Grand Pier at Weston-super-Mare, Wedmore Harvest Home, Bristol Colston Hall, the Cleeve Cider Festival and the Great Dorset Steam Fair among them, and it must be said that big outdoor events are still a speciality. After all, what's a West Country knees-up without the Wurzels?

As he promised immediately after Adge's death, their manager John Miles steered them to a number one hit with *Combine Harvester* in 1976, and they followed it up with *I am a Cider Drinker* later the same year and *Farmer Bill's Cowman,* which narrowly missed reaching the Top Thirty the following year. 'It was a couple of years after Adge's death that Bob Barratt rang me, saying he'd heard a guy in Ireland had written some sort of parody of *Brand New Key,*' says John. 'He sent it to me, the Wurzels changed it a bit, and we released it as *Combine Harvester.* For me, this was an opportunity to fulfil my promise to them. We got to number three, but they were so exhausted with promoting it that they said "John, we'll never hold this against you, let's settle for this." I rang Noel Edmonds and told him about it and asked him to look kindly on it for the *Radio One Roadshow,* which was in the West Country the following week. He said "Yeah, I'll give it a play," and when he heard it he said "Yeah, it's good fun, I'll give it a play on Wednesday." I said Noel, I thought you were going to play it every day. Why not? Play it on Monday. Everybody will love it. You see. And bless him, he did, and lots of the Roadshow's twelve or thirteen million listeners did love it, and all the other DJs took it up and it just went on from there.'

Brand New Key had been a hit four years previously for Melanie Safka, an off-beat American singer-songwriter who simply called herself Melanie on her records. Lots of people were baffled by the words of *Brand New Key*, brand new roller skates and all, but she denied the imagery was particularly obscure. 'I wrote it in about fifteen minutes one night,' she said. 'I thought it was cute, a kind of old Thirties tune. I guess a key and a lock have always been Freudian symbols, and pretty obvious ones at that. There was no deep serious expression behind the song, but people read things into it.' Perhaps part of the problem was that while old Sigmund might have had plenty to say about keys and locks, he seems to have kept pretty schtum about keys and roller skates. Anyway, by the time the song had been Wurzelised it didn't really matter.

Combine Harvester and *I am a Cider Drinker* saw the post-Adge Wurzels at their peak, with Pete Budd playing the cheeky chappie to perfection. To see the personification of one of those randy, leering Donald McGill comic postcard commercial travellers or door-to-door salesmen, just tune in to Pete on the *Top of the Pops* video of *Combine Harvester*. You see it on telly often enough, accompanied by right-on, pofaced critics expounding on how far-removed and out of touch *TOTP* had become from the Punk youth culture of 1976. Yes, but all the show was really doing was what it said it was doing, and showcasing the biggest hits of the time. The best-selling record of 1976 was Brotherhood of Man's *Save Your Kisses for Me*, and other artists in the year's Top Ten included Abba twice, Dr Hook, Chicago, Tina Charles, Demis Roussos and the Four Seasons. You could argue that *Combine Harvester* was hip and cutting-edge in comparison with most of that lot; whatever it was, in the first of its two weeks at number one, on June 12 1976, it kept Wings' *Silly Love Songs* off the top of the charts, and it would be nice to think Paul McCartney saw the irony in that.

And where would Adge be today with the Wurzels? 'I'd love to think he'd still be writing great songs for us, but I'm sure he wouldn't be playing, quite apart from the fact that he would have turned eighty in November 2011,' says Tommy Banner. 'The style of the band has changed a lot since his day with a more contemporary feel led by drum and bass, and he wouldn't have been happy with that. He couldn't have coped with a drummer; he used to jump bars, miss a verse out and apart from this, I don't think that for several years past he'd have been able to keep up with our schedule, even as it is today. I can't think of anything much he wrote in his later years, other than *Up the Clump* and *Aloha, Severn Beach*, but if he'd had more time to dedicate to writing, who knows? Yes, if he could still be here writing songs for us: that would be magic.'

Adge songs that feature regularly in the Wurzels' schedule are *Champion Dung Spreader, Shepton Mallet Matador, All Over Mendip* and *Pill, Pill*. There's another one that's performed every time as the last rabble-rousing encore, and readers of this book need no reminding which that one is.

It was in 1987 when John Miles and the Wurzels parted company, and now John makes a startling admission. 'I think leaving them was the biggest mistake I ever made,' he says. 'I was looking after all these other acts, and it was hard work keeping the Wurzels working. My enthusiasm at that point was waning, and I felt that theirs was, too, going over the old songs, not liking rehearsing. I told Tommy I wasn't really booking clubs at that stage, and said I felt Wally Dent would be a good guy for them to go to. Wally felt the same, so they went to him. But I wish I hadn't parted company with them. I was stale, but if I could have had just a year off, just a break, we could have come back all the stronger.' The Wurzels went through one or two managerial changes in what can be looked back on as their fallow years, but now have another winner in Sil Willcox. Their only enemy now is *Anno Domini*.

What will never go away in the foreseeable future is the Scrumpy and Western tradition Adge has left behind. Two prominent West Country bands emerged at much the same time as the Wurzels – the Yetties from Dorset in 1967 and Shag Connors and the Carrot Crunchers from Gloucestershire a little later, and while the Yetties can be seen as another act from the booming folk scene whose success owed little to Adge, the Carrot Crunchers were very much a Wurzels soundalike in their early days. That said, Mick Connors was a considerable song writer in his own right, and he had a marvellous gimmick in a cockerel that used to come on stage with him and drink beer. The band is still working hard as Mart Connors and the Carrot Crunchers under Mick's son Martin. Mick died in 1987 after a long fight against cancer.

A few years ago the *Wurzelmania* website published a list of scores of bands and acts that owe their existence to Adge. Several of these will doubtless no longer be with us, while it is equally likely that new ones have taken their place. You hear it said often enough that some of the best of the tribute bands are more authentic to the original sound than the present-day Wurzels are, and that is true. Most of the acts are groups of enthusiasts who come together perhaps once a week – 'Saving it up for Friday night', as Mark Knopfler had it in *Sultans of Swing* – while for the Wurzels it has been the no small matter of selling themselves and keeping some kind of pace with the musical trends of these past nigh-on fifty years. Among the most prominent bands are the splendidly named Mangled Wurzels from East Somerset and the Cornish Wurzells, who have a genuine ex-Wurzel, Terry Pascoe, in their ranks. Other names in the list that catch the eye include the Cowshed Cleaners from Tiverton, the Cutlers of Cornwall, Twurzel, Combyne Arvester, the Plonkers Agricultural Orchestra from the New Forest, Surfin' Turnips, the Somerset Paddies, More Silage, the Swinging Udders from Bath, Midsomer Norton's finest, the Scrumpy Bashers and the Somerset Barnstormers.

It was the Cornish Wurzells who tried to launch an appeal for a life-sized statue of Adge to be put up in Nailsea in 2011; raising £40,000 for such a project is no mean undertaking and first time around they did not get very far, but there already exists the perfect model for any future statue in a splendid bronzed resin work some four feet tall created by Roy Cleeves, a retired builder who went to Old Church School at around the time Adge left, and is still in touch with various members of the family, including Dave Cutler. Roy has modelled his statue on the image of Adge on the cover of the first LP, *Adge Cutler and the Wurzels*, and has created a remarkable facial likeness despite having had no formal artistic training. In the meantime, in October 2012 Nailsea Town Council was about to place a metal bench incorporating a two-dimension image of Adge in the town centre, along with others commemorating the social reformer Hannah More and the cider maker Redvers Coate.

One means of celebrating Adge that sadly is unlikely to take off is the renaming of Bristol Airport after him, in the tradition of George Best at Dublin and John Lennon at Liverpool. Calls for such a move came in August 2009 when a jokey Facebook campaign was begun by Phil Brockwell, head of a private jet hire firm based at the airport. 'Adge is Somerset's answer to Jimmy Dean, a legend cut off in his prime,' said Phil, and the Bristol papers sat up and took notice. Well, you know what a slow news month August can be...

Meanwhile, our hero's memory lives on all over the country in numerous other Mr Cutlers who find themselves blessed with the nickname Adge. Introducing Paul 'Adge' Cutler late of the Survey Ships Association, Ian 'Adge' Cutler, a Scot who writes books about Hull Kingston Rovers Rugby League club, Adge Cutler the Star Trek fan, Sergeant Adge Cutler of the Royal Marines Band, just plain Mr Adge Cutler of the Old West Bromwich Photos Society... Desperately disappointingly, the baby names website still has no place for Adge, but it is surely only a matter of time.

He can certainly still crop up in some unusual places, not least, in November 2011, in the high-powered American *Forbes Magazine*, which specialises in business and finance. Its contributor Tim Worstall, in a piece titled *Decline in the Fine Arts or the Sieve of History?*, argued that we should not be worried by suggestions that art forms such as literature and classical music are said to be becoming increasingly irrelevant in most students' cultural lives. 'I'm afraid that this is nonsense...' he wrote. 'The common culture has always been, well, common. An Eighteenth-century Englishman did not wander around singing Handel arias... The actual songs that were sung were dreary things like *God Save the King* (originally from a musical) or the usual *I Had my Mangles Wurzled by the Milkmaid* common to all rural societies when drink has been taken and sex is being alluded to. The Twentieth century did not find hysterical crowds screaming for an encore of Sir Harrison Birtwhistle's latest (although there have been reports of screaming hysteria at being forced to attend another performance) but they did buy up lorry loads of *Drink Up Thy Zider* by Adge Cutler and the Wurzels. Quite rightly too, good song, nothing at all to do with it being the local anthem of my home area.'

Time and again, old friends and acquaintances of Adge have remarked that, when meeting him at the height of his fame, they were struck by how he remained the man they had known. Terry Elverd: 'Last time I saw him was in a café in Bath Road in Bristol, near where I was working. Life had changed quite a bit for both of us since our young days but he was still the same, full of jokes and fun, still Adge as I had ever known him.' Hector Hamer: 'The last time I saw Adge was at a barbecue on a farm at Farrington Gurney, where he was appearing with Acker Bilk. I went over, we shook hands, and I was able to tell him it was more than a pleasure to see him doing so well. He was still the same as ever.' George Dimond: 'The last time we saw him was when we went to Weymouth for a trip, and there was his name up in lights outside the Pavilion. By chance, he was standing outside talking to some people, but as soon as he spotted us he was on to us in a flash. "George! Come for a pint, mate..." Everyone says it, and it's true. He never changed.'

What is equally striking is the number of people, mainly men, it must be said, who take an intense interest in Adge and all his works, despite being only children or in some cases not even born when his career came to its tragic end. Luke Hebden, an avid admirer still in his twenties, has extensive files and notes on his hero's career, but surely his most impressive declaration of allegiance is an Adge Cutler tattoo over his heart, the great man's face smiling out from his chest in an image copied extremely faithfully from the cover of the *Don't Tell I, Tell 'Ee* LP, the photograph taken outside the Black Horse at Clapton-in-Gordano.

Michael Ansell, who lives close to Adge's old home at Tickenham Hill, is another young man steeped in Wurzels lore. 'When I was young I went with my father to Weston-super-Mare library, where they were selling off records from the stock they lent out,' he says. 'We pulled out that record made when the window was smashed [*Adge Cutler's Family Album*], washed it in Fairy Liquid and played it till it wore out. I've been hooked on the Wurzels since I was nine, and I'm now forty-three! I've seen them so often in concert, and once I even came into close contact with Tommy Banner. When I was at Churchill School I went for work experience to a recording studio in Cave Street, St Paul's, and Tommy came in on my second day, when they were remixing a song. He asked me to go and make him a cup of tea. He seemed to think that was what work experience people were for. I thought there was more to it than that, but who was I to argue with a Wurzel?'

And then there is Jonathan Conibere, surely the most avid and committed of them all, contributor at different times to both the major Wurzels websites and a meticulous compiler of facts, figures and arcane details. His quest to put together the definitive Wurzels discography is on-going and in the ever-expanding range of its ambition, potentially never-ending.

As this book went to print, he and the author were speculating on the contents of various recordings, including a seven-inch 45rpm EP newly discovered by Adge's stepdaughter Su Elliott in a suitcase full of her mother Yvonne's belongings. It is a demo put on vinyl by the Record Centre at 5, Denmark Street, Bristol, and written on the A-side in Adge's hand, complete with great blob of ink, is '*Drink Up Thee Zider/ Easton-in-Gordano* at Royal Oak, Nailsea, 1958'. Yes, 1958, eight years before the legendary recording of the song at that venue, and at a time when he was still labouring at Portishead B. The flipside is equally intriguing, labelled in what looks to be somebody else's hand: *'In the Haymaking Time* (with Acker)'. What delights will they hold, these earliest known recordings of Adge as an out-and-out amateur? That remains to be heard, but if the outcome is a new Adge Cutler single after thirty-eight years, that will be riches indeed to add to the legacy.

DISCOGRAPHY

Single: Drink Up Thy Zider/ Twice Daily (Columbia DB 8081, 1966)

EP: *Scrumpy & Western* (Columbia SEG 8525, 1967)
Side one
1 Pill, Pill
2 Twice Daily
Side two
3 Hark at 'Ee Jacko
4 Drink Up Thy Zider

Album: *Adge Cutler and the Wurzels* (Columbia SX 6126, 1967, reissued in duophonic, Columbia SCX 6126, 1976, CD Absolute, CIA 007, 2009). Recorded live at the Royal Oak, Nailsea
Side one
1 Twice Daily
2 Tanglefoot Twitch
3 When The Common Market Comes To Stanton Drew
4 Thee Cassn't Kill Cooch
5 The Champion Dung Spreader
6 Drink Up Thy Zider
Side two
1 Pill, Pill
2 Mabel, Mabel
3 The Chew Magna Cha-Cha
4 Hark at 'Ee Jacko
5 The Mixer Man's Lament
6 Virtute Et Industrial

Single: The Champion Dung Spreader/ When the Common Market comes to Stanton Drew (Columbia DB 8145, 1967)

Single: I Wish I Was Back On The Farm/Easton-in-Gordano (Columbia DB 8222, 1967)

Album: *Adge Cutler's Family Album* (Columbia SX 6165, 1967, reissued in duophonic, Columbia SCX 6165, 1976, CD Absolute, CIA 008, 2009). Recorded live at the Royal Oak, Nailsea

Side one

1 Easton-in-Gordano
2 Sweet Violets
3 The Wild West Show
4 Barcelona Blues
5 The Somerset Space Race
6 Freak-Out In Somerset

Side two

1 Moonlight On The Malago
2 Sniff Up Thy Snuff
3 Drunk Again
4 Sheriff Of Midsomer Norton
5 Avonmouth Mary
6 The Shepton Mallet Matador

Single: All Over Mendip/My Threshing Machine (Columbia DB 8277, 1967)

Single: Don't Tell I, Tell 'Ee/Faggots Is the Stuff (Columbia DB 8399, 1968)

Single: Up The Clump/Aloha, Severn Beach (Columbia DB 8462, 1968)

Album: *Cutler of the West* (Columbia SX 6263 mono, SCX 6263 stereo, both 1968, reissued in duophonic, Columbia SCX 6263, 1976, CD EMI Gold 5-84807-1-6, 2003; reissued in stereo as *Vintage Cider*, Music For Pleasure MFP 50476, 1980). Recorded live at the Webbington Country Club, Loxton and the White Buck Inn, Burley, Hampshire

Side one

1 Drink Up Thy Zider (play-on)

2 The Charlton Mackrell Jug Band

3 In The Haymaking Time

4 Five Foot Flirt

5 Thee's Got'n Where Thee Cassn't Back'n, Hassn't?

6 Dorset Is Beautiful

7 Up The Clump

Side two

1 Drink Up Thy Zider (play-on)

2 The Chandler's Wife

3 The Bristol Song

4 The Marrow Song (Oh! What A Beauty)

5 A Pub With No Beer

6 Oh! Sir Jasper

7 The Wurple-Diddle-I-Doo-Song (The Village Band)

8 Drink Up Thy Zider (play-off)

Single: Ferry to Glastonbury/Saturday Night at the Crown (Columbia DB 8614)

Album: *Carry On Cutler* (Columbia SX 6367 mono, Columbia SCX 6367 stereo, 1969, reissued duophonic SCX 6367, 1976, CD Absolute, CIA 009, 2009) Recorded live at the Webbington Country Club, Loxton and the White Buck Inn, Burley, Hampshire

Side one
1 Drink Up Thy Zider (play-on)
2 All Over Mendip
3 Down On The Farm
4 Folk Song
5 Aloha, Severn Beach
6 Oom Pah Pah (from *Oliver*)
7 Harvest Of Love

Side two
1 I Couldn't Spell !!**&@&**!!
2 Chewton Mendip Love-In
3 Saturday Night At The Crown
4 Riley's Cow-Shed
5 Ferry To Glastonbury
6 Willie The Shake
7 Drink Up Thy Zider

Single: Poor Poor Farmer/Chitterling (Columbia DB 8793, 1971)

Single: Little Darlin'/Mother Nature Calling (CBS 8067, 1972)

Album: *Don't Tell I, Tell 'Ee* (EMI Starline, SRS 5119, 1972, CD Absolute, CIA 010, 2009)

Side one
1 Drink Up Thy Zider (play-on)
2 Don't Tell I, Tell 'Ee

3 Oom Pah Pah (from Oliver)

4 Poor, Poor Farmer

5 Chitterling

6 My Threshing Machine

7 I Wish I Was Back On The Farm

Side two

 1 The Wild West Show

2 I'd Love To Swim In The Zuider Zee

3 Faggots Is The Stuff

4 Virtute Et Industrial

5 The Wurple-Diddle-I-Doo Song (The Village Band)

6 Drink Up Thy Zider (play-off)

Single: Drink Up Thy Zider/Twice Daily (Columbia DB9031, 1974, reissue of DB8081)

Single: Little Darlin'/Mother Nature Calling (Santa Ponsa PNS 20, 1974, reissue of CBS 8067)

Album: *The Very Best of Adge Cutler* (EMI EMC 3191, 1977, reissued as *Cider Drinking Favourites*, EMI Notes NTS 199, 1980)

Side one

1 Easton-in-Gordano

2 Poor, Poor Farmer

3 Twice Daily

4 The Wurple-Diddle-I-Doo Song

5 Don't Tell I, Tell 'Ee

6 Saturday Night At The Crown

7 Riley's Cowshed

8 Ferry To Glastonbury

9 Up The Clump

Side two

1 Thee's Got'n Where Thee Cassn't Back'n, Hassn't?

2 Moonlight On The Malago

3 The Shepton Mallet Matador

4 When The Common Market Comes To Stanton Drew

5 The Champion Dung Spreader

6 Aloha, Severn Beach

7 All Over Mendip

8 I Wish I Was Back On The Farm

9 Drink Up Thy Zider

Album: *Don't Tell I, Tell 'Ee* (EMI Encore, ONCR 502, 1978)

Side one

1 Drink Up Thy Zider (play-on)

2 Don't Tell I, Tell 'Ee

3 Oom Pah Pah (from *Oliver*)

4 Poor, Poor Farmer

5 Chitterling

6 My Threshing Machine

7 I Wish I Was Back On The Farm

8 Dorset Is Beautiful

9 Up The Clump

Side two

1 The Wild West Show

2 I'd Love To Swim In The Zuider Zee

3. Faggots Is The Stuff

4. Virtute Et Industrial

5. The Wurple-Diddle-I-Doo Song (The Village Band)

6. The Chandler's Wife

7. Drink Up Thy Zider (play-off)

The album ***The Wurzels are Scrumptious*** (EMI One-Up OU 2087, 1975, CD CIA011 Absolute, 2009) contains two previously unreleased Adge Cutler songs: *Look At 'Ee Lookin' At I* (written with Henry Davis) and *I'm the Captain of a Dredger,* both written with Henry Davis.

The album ***The Combine Harvester*** by The Wurzels (EMI One-Up OU2138, 1976) contains the previously unreleased Adge Cutler song *Down in Nempnett Thrubwell.*

All twelve tracks of side two of the album ***The Wurzels and Adge Cutler and the Wurzels*** (EMI Ideal CDP 7 96080 2, 1991) feature Adge Cutler and the Wurzels.

Six tracks of the CD album ***The Finest 'Arvest of The Wurzels and Adge Cutler*** (EMI Gold 527 0462) are written by Adge Cutler, and several others are performed by him.

Five of the twenty-one tracks of the CD album ***The Wurzels' Greatest Hits*** (EMI Gold 0946-3-93902-2-9, 2007) are written by Adge Cutler.

ACKNOWLEDGMENTS

The author gives his grateful thanks to all who have contributed to this book, principal among whom are David Cutler, Roy Cutler, Tommy Banner, Pete Budd, Michael Ansell, Geraldine Box, Keith Box, Gerry Brooke, Clive Burlton, Royston Cleeves, Jonathan Conibere, HM Coroner, Newport, Ted Cowell, Tim Davey, Grace Davies, Henry Davies, John Dunmore, Su Elliott, Barbara Elverd, Terry Elverd, Stephen Elverd, Maurice Fells, Keith Gissing, Pat Gordon, the late Melvyn Gordon, Gwent Archives at Ebbw Vale, Mervyn Hancock, Hector Hamer, Trudy Hamer, Roland Harmer, Luke Hebden, the *Hereford Times*, Haydn James, Chris Jones, Dave Jones of Cavern City Tours, Liverpool, Mark Jones, Cecil Keel, Ann Kingston, Andy Leggett, Peggy Lloyd, Norman Lott, Gef Lucena, John Macey, John Miles, Janet Miller, Quita Morgan, Philip Morris, John Mortimer, Julia Berridge and Ceri Manton at Nailsea Library, the *Nailsea, Clevedon and Portishead Times,* Alex Jarvis and Ryan Pimm at Newport Reference Library, Bernard Petteford, Howard Rudman, Kathy Shortman, Pete Shutler, Richard Simmons, Peter Skuse, Coreen Stone, Jean Taylor, David and Greta Thrush, John Tucker, Robert Tucker, Rosalyn Wade, Brian Walker, Charles Wallace, Sue Wedlock, Tom White, the Wiltshire and Swindon History Centre at Chippenham and John Woodhams.

PICTURE CREDITS

Photographs in this book are by courtesy of Su Elliott, Jonathan Conibere, John Miles, Bedminster Down Boys' Club, Royston Cleeves, Terry Elverd, Luke Hebden, Haydn James, Andy Leggett, Derek Paget, Coreen Stone, David and Greta Thrush, Rosalyn Wade, the Wiltshire and Swindon History Centre at Chippenham and John Woodhams, with all due acknowledgment to copyright holders.

BIBLIOGRAPHY AND WEBSITES

Wurzel's World, by Mervyn Hancock, Western Daily Press, 2004

Bristol Folk, by Mark Jones, Bristol Folk Publications, 2009

The Saydisc and Village Thing Discography, by Mark Jones, Bristol Folk Publications, 2009

www.thewurzels.com

www.wurzelmania.co.uk